The
Incredible
Great
White
Fleet

The Incredible Great White Fleet

Samuel Carter III

CROWELL-COLLIER PRESS / NEW YORK
COLLIER-MACMILLAN LIMITED / LONDON

For George A. Huhn
Commodore of gallant record

Library of Congress Catalog Card Number: 77–129747

The Macmillan Company
866 Third Avenue
New York, New York 10022

Collier-Macmillan Canada Ltd., Toronto, Ontario

Printed in the United States of America

10 9 8 7 6 5 4 3 2 1

PICTURE CREDITS

Culver Pictures, Inc., 12, 20, 76
Department of the Navy, Naval Photographic Center,
        52–53, 116–17, 141, 157, 171
Historical Pictures Service—Chicago, title page
Navy Department in the National Archives, 99

Contents

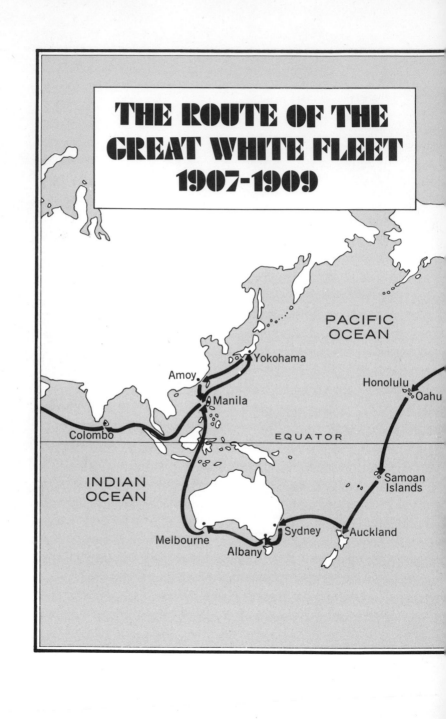

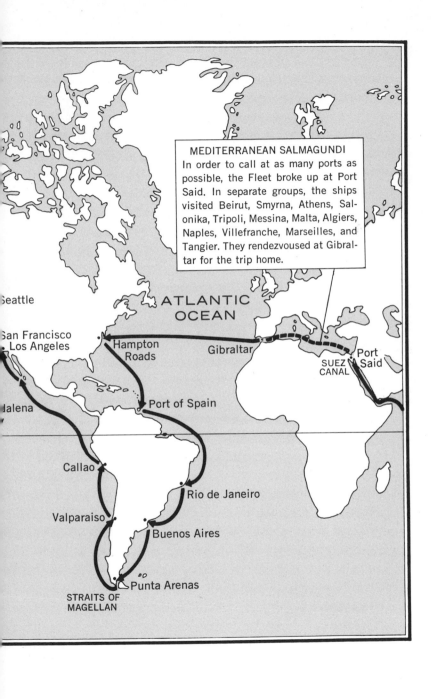

MEDITERRANEAN SALMAGUNDI
In order to call at as many ports as possible, the Fleet broke up at Port Said. In separate groups, the ships visited Beirut, Smyrna, Athens, Salonika, Tripoli, Messina, Malta, Algiers, Naples, Villefranche, Marseilles, and Tangier. They rendezvoused at Gibraltar for the trip home.

ATLANTIC OCEAN

Seattle

San Francisco
Los Angeles

Hampton Roads

Gibraltar

Port Said

SUEZ CANAL

Jalena

Port of Spain

Callao

Rio de Janeiro

Valparaiso

Buenos Aires

Punta Arenas

STRAITS OF MAGELLAN

1

▶

Prelude to History

▶
▶

For three days it had rained in torrents and a near gale wind had lashed the waters of Hampton Roads, Virginia. But now on the morning of December 16, 1907, the skies were clear and a bright sun shone on an awe-inspiring spectacle such as few before had ever witnessed. " 'Twould perhaps be worth ten years of peaceful life, one glance at that array," quoted a poetic news reporter. Sixteen snow-white battleships, guns and brass gleaming, signal flags whipping in the breeze, stretched in a double line from Fort Munroe to the open sea a mile away—straining like bulldogs at their leashes to set forth on an epoch-making journey.

Their declared destination: fourteen thousand miles to San Francisco, though rumor had it they would press on clear around the world. Their ostensible purpose: to allay the fear of Californians that their coast was threatened by Japanese invasion and to convince Japan that she no longer dominated the Pacific. There were other goals, however. Among them, to impress the world with America's new-found naval might and secure for this country its just role as a power among nations; and, too, to stimulate public interest in the navy, and to win support for the still unfinished Panama Canal.

The statistics of that mighty fleet defied imagination. Some quarter of a million tons made up the combined displacement of the ships, more than amassed by Nelson at the battle of Trafalgar. Nearly a hundred million dollars had been spent in its construction. With thirty-five million tons of ammunition in the magazines, and a thousand guns to hurl it at the target, it was five times more powerful than any fleet America had yet assembled.

"No one in these last hours is aware of the massive destruction power of that fleet," wrote John Scott Merriweather, a Roosevelt-selected correspondent who accompanied the fleet. "The bands play, the ladies and gentlemen promenade and talk, the bluejackets make merry during their last hours in a home port—and all this time the ships are ready to let loose a storm of destruction such as never before was wrought by man on the face of the waters."

But destruction was not the theme of those last hours of farewell at Hampton Roads. It seemed as if half America had come to see the ships depart. "Ain't seen so many folks out since the *Merrimac* fought the *Monitor* right here in 1862," a hinterland farmer volunteered. Hundreds of excursion boats and bunting-bedecked pleasure craft swarmed about the floating battlewagons. Cliffs and beaches were black with spectators, while the veranda and roof of the Chamberlin Hotel, which had entertained the ensigns and their sweethearts at a ball the night before, were jammed with handkerchief-waving navy wives and sweethearts.

From the ships' decks glittering marine bands serenaded the responsive throng with repeated strains of "The Girl I Left Behind Me."

Between the double line of ships rode the presidential yacht, down from Washington to review the fleet and offer the president's farewell. With his naval aide, Commander William Sowden Sims beside him, Theodore Roosevelt climbed to the *Mayflower*'s bridge, jaws set and expression resolute, one hand guarding his high silk hat against the wind. "By George!" he was heard to exclaim above the furor, "Did you ever see such a day and such a fleet!"

The man upon the bridge *is* the Great White Fleet, its soul and spirit, and the father of this undertaking. Sickly from birth he had overcome infirmity with a life of action and robust variety and had entered politics when only two years out of Harvard. Through a series of governmental offices he rose to become assistant secretary of the navy under President McKinley.

Of all roles to date this suited him most perfectly. He had been imbued with a sense of glory in the navy by two uncles who had served with distinction on Confederate warships in the Civil War. He brought to his office an excess of zeal. In 1898 it was Roosevelt who, in the absence of his superior, ordered Admiral Dewey to Manila to intercept the Spanish fleet should war break out with Spain. And it was Roosevelt who, according to more than one historian, did more to bring the United States Navy to its full potential than any American before him.

Returning a hero from the war with Spain, in which he resigned his naval office for service with the troops, he was elected governor of New York State and then vice-president of the United States when William McKinley was elected to a second term. With McKinley's assassination in September, 1901, young Roosevelt, only forty-two, succeeded to the highest office in the land.

He was singularly right for the office and the time, a man of the people yet a product of aristocratic breeding. Individualistic, domineering, and at times belligerent, he believed in himself unequivocally as a spokesman for America. More than that, he believed unequivocally in America. Relentlessly he battled for reform in its domestic affairs, but equally relentlessly he battled for America's authority in global politics. He aroused the country from its sense of isolation to an active role among the powers of the world.

America was ripe for such a president. The boom of industrialization had given the nation a sense of power and a restless itch about its future. The term "manifest destiny" was heard across the land, a term applying to the right of the United States to extend its influence and boundaries to those areas surrounding it—the Caribbean and Pacific islands, even Canada—which might be profitably exploited. While there were those who deplored this unfamiliar trend towards imperialism it was a trend that, at the turn of the century, engulfed the world.

Throughout Europe, nationalism and expansion were the watchwords of the era. With the mightiest navy in the world, Great Britain patrolled a global circuit of possessions. France and Germany vied for interests in the Pacific and North Africa. Russia aspired to control Manchuria and Mongolia. These territorial designs were backed by rising armaments and growing navies as the chess game for colonial expansion spread. It called for protective treaties and commitments. Germany, Italy, and Austria formed the Grand Alliance; England, France, and Russia formed the Triple Entente. These were almost supernations, poised in a delicate balance of power, armed to the teeth against each other. Only the United States was free of such entanglements—free to make its own decisions.

In the Orient, where China struggled to contain its sheer enormity, one power stood supreme: Japan. Though an ally of Great Britain, which had condoned her recent war with Russia, Japan was a lonely giant in Pacific waters. Ambitious, touchy, envious of her Western neighbors, she had grown in stature mightily since her doors were opened to the world by Commodore Matthew Perry in 1854. She now possessed the world's fourth largest navy, following those of Britain, France, and the United States.

It was the German Kaiser Wilhelm II who coined the phrase "Yellow Peril" to define Japan's ambitions after its defeat of Russia in 1904–05. It was a phrase that for West Coast Americans had ominous significance. Japanese invasion of that coast was so far one of peaceful immigration, but where would it end? Though still a minority, the Japanese seemed everywhere, in labor, trade, and business. In California particularly, fear and resentment of the Oriental led to racial persecution and discrimination.

In Japan these feelings were reciprocated. Smarting from Roosevelt's settlement of the Russo-Japanese war, which denied reparation payments to Japan, the Japanese viewed their Pacific neighbor with suspicion and distrust. Among other abuses which the Japanese had suffered in America were the barring of Japanese students from the schools of San Francisco and anti-Japanese riots in the streets. "Stand up, Japanese nation," cried the Tokyo press. "Our countrymen have been humiliated on the other side of the Pacific. . . . We should be ready to give a blow to the United States."

In world opinion, war between Japan and the United States was a foregone conclusion. The British Admiralty was betting five to four that the Japanese would be victorious. A widely circulated German novel, *Banzai,* related how the Japanese navy wiped out the American navy in an hour and invaded California. President Roosevelt distrusted jingoism, but he was aware of the existing threat. "My own judgment is," he said, "that the only thing which will prevent war is the Japanese feeling that we shall not be beaten." Sending a strong fleet to the Pacific was one way to promote that feeling.

Such battleship diplomacy was far from new. In fact the battleship had become an emblem of prestige throughout the world. In a period when "glory" was a word to be used without embarrassment, the warship was synonymous with glory. "A great battleship is the noblest work of man," wrote Henry Wadsworth Longfellow. Nations vied with one another in staging gala naval reviews and battleship parades, to raise the blood of their peoples and impress their neighbors. And the queens of these carnivals were the battleships—"my darlings," the German kaiser called them—the thorny symbols of a nation's might and a warning to her rivals.

It was not Roosevelt alone who had raised the American navy from its nadir following the Civil War to its present 1907 strength. A convincing naval officer, Alfred Thayer Mahan, published in 1890 a volume called *The Influence of Sea Power on History* which postulated that control of the oceans was the key to national supremacy. Both Grover Cleveland's secretary of the navy, William C. White, and later Assistant Secretary Roosevelt came under Mahan's spell, and in 1890 the navy began to build—four 10,000-ton class battleships as a starter, followed by the sixteen which comprised the white armada. In a review of his reconstituted fleet Roosevelt exclaimed, "Oh, Lord! if only the people who are ignorant about our Navy could see these great warships in all their majesty, and could realize how well fitted they are to uphold the honor of America!" That was one of the responsibilities, not only to have a navy but to show it to the public and the world.

Just when Roosevelt conceived his idea for a cruise to the Pacific is hard to say. Perhaps it stemmed from 1905 when Japan's defeat of the Russian navy in a crushing show of force convinced him that America's strength in the Pacific should be bolstered. And why stop at the Pacific? What more impressive evidence of the country's new-found stature than to put these battlewagons on display around the world, calling on foreign ports to flex their muscles. Not only Japan would take the hint, but Europe too.

This was not his openly expressed objective. It was to be ostensibly a good-will cruise providing naval practice and experience. "The best place," wrote Roosevelt, "for a naval officer to learn his duties is at sea, by performing them, and only by actually putting through a voyage of this nature, a voyage longer than ever before undertaken by so large a fleet, can we find out just exactly what is necessary for us to know as to our naval needs." That the American people might take pride in such initiative, support appropriations for the navy and the not-yet-finished Panama Canal, were other benefits to be derived.

On the announcement of his plan to send the fleet to the Pacific there were sharp reactions. Many in Congress viewed it as a wasteful gesture, signifying nothing. And there were those who regarded it as an unwarranted expression of belligerency—Roosevelt's "Big Stick" afloat. *Harper's Weekly* called it an "extravagant display of force" which caused uneasiness among its readers. Mark Twain wrote that it was "all for show," to make a great noise that would satisfy the president. But to Americans at large, who were caught in the battleship spell, it was, as one reporter put it, "Uncle Sam's Greatest Show on Earth."

Abroad, the cruise was regarded with misgiving. England's *St. James Gazette* considered it "a bombastic exhibit of naval strength for the sake of intimidating Japan." The London *Spectator* called it "most untimely because it excites the jingo spirit." The French press regarded it as a warmongering gesture, asking: "Is the magnificent fleet being watched by the Japanese from some dangerous ambush? Will Admiral Evans, when he arrives in April or May, find the Japanese already occupying Hawaii or the Philippines?"

Only in Germany was the venture viewed with satisfaction. Kaiser Wilhelm II, smarting under the arrogance of

Britain's navy and surrounded by the Triple Entente, hoped for an alliance with America to even up the power balance. He saw the White Fleet's cruise as provocative; perhaps it *would* lead to conflict with Japan. If so, he reasoned, the untested fleet would be defeated, and the United States would be forced into the arms of Germany for her salvation.

Some home strategists observed that, with the Battle Fleet in the Pacific, the whole North Atlantic and the East Coast would be stripped of its defenses. Others deplored the risk of sending such a major portion of the navy into unfamiliar waters far from its home bases. Roosevelt, however, had the implied assurance of Germany that she would stand by to protect the North Atlantic. He felt, too, that Japan was too depleted from her war with Russia to attempt, so soon, another war with the United States.

Japan itself seemed anxious to allay this talk of war. In Tokyo the *Jiji Shimpo,* an independent paper, hailed the "noteworthy undertaking." "We do not entertain the idea even for a moment that the purpose of the trip is to threaten Japan. Should the American fleet visit these shores, it will be greeted by a most cordial reception." But it warned, in an underlying note of uneasiness, against any further anti-Japanese movements on the West Coast "similar to the regrettable incident in San Francisco." A barrage of press opinions about the cruise was also given in America's leading journals. "The presence of an American fleet in the Pacific is more likely to prevent war than precipitate it." "We shall have proved to the satisfaction of all well-informed onlookers that, in a superlative sense, we are a great world power even in an ocean which for us is the most difficult of access." "Chinese statesmen will be encouraged to resist the encroachment of the Japanese on Chinese sovereign territory. . . ."

The latter postulation was linked to the belief that "the evident purpose of Japan is ultimately to control China as she now controls Korea." This in turn was linked to another widely held belief. "Japan will soon control the trade of the Pacific. Her merchant fleet is growing with great rapidity, not only in the American traffic, but in the commerce of Korea, Formosa, China, India, and the Far East generally." In short, American optimists, suggested *Harper's Weekly,* had better revise their opinion that "the Pacific will always be dominated by the United States," unless the navy was prepared to back that statement.

Japan was the bogey on the high seas as she was to the uneasy citizens of California. Her fleet boasted only thirteen battleships compared with twenty-six for the United States. But she had marked superiority in lighter, swifter vessels, with fifty-seven destroyers and seventy-nine torpedo boats. Not only that but her naval strategy and fire power—as evidenced in her victory over Russia—were not to be taken lightly.

How did Japan herself regard the cruise? In his embassy in Washington, Baron Kogoro Takahira announced, "We have no reason to be suspicious about the visit of the Atlantic Fleet to the Pacific; it is purely an American affair." Besides, as Roosevelt had duly noted, Japan was actively preparing for the World Exposition to be held in Tokyo in 1912. She had, presumably, other things to think about.

Nevertheless, a principal objective of the Pacific cruise was to reassure the West Coast that the country's navy was concerned with its defense, as well as to impress Japan with America's naval power and mobility. Roosevelt himself had nothing against the Japanese; and he did not subscribe to the idea of inevitable war between the two Pacific naval powers. However, it wouldn't hurt to give Japan a warning. His was the admonition, "Speak softly, and carry a big stick; you will go far." Roosevelt's big stick was the navy.

Typically, Roosevelt paid little heed to Congress or his Cabinet in planning for the voyage. "I determined to move without consulting the Cabinet precisely as I took Panama without consulting the Cabinet." Nor did he consult Congress on his secret plan to send the fleet around the world. His jocular intent was, I shall get them going and let Congress worry about how to bring them back. In midsummer he met with his naval advisers to arrange the details of the expedition. Its announced itinerary:

Assemble Hampton Roads	Dec. 9
Trinidad, B. W. I.	Dec. 24
Rio de Janeiro, Brazil	Jan. 11
Punta Arenas, Chile	Jan. 31
Callao, Peru	Feb. 18
Magdalena Bay, Mexico	May 14

No date was set for arrival in California. Nor was it officially revealed that San Francisco was a halfway point. The president had only stated enigmatically: "The question

of the route by which the fleet returns has not yet been decided." However, the *New York Times* observed, even before the ships' departure: "It has been repeatedly reported that the fleet might eventually circle the globe, some color being given to the report by the fact that the Navy Department has furnished the navigator of each ship with corrected charts showing the way from San Francisco to Manila and Gibraltar."

Of the twenty-six battleships in the United States Navy, the president had counted on twenty to make up the cruise. But four were considered unequal to the expedition, and he was forced to settle for sixteen. They were not then called the Great White Fleet, but rather the Atlantic Fleet or Battle Fleet—the more descriptive appellation would come later. A flotilla of six torpedo boats would screen the fleet and act as escorts, and these would be dispatched in advance to Trinidad. Four auxiliaries would accompany the battleships, plus the waspish *Yankton,* a converted yacht to be used for ceremonial occasions.

Coaling was a prime consideration. According to Mahan, a fleet was as strong as its supply of coal. Nearly a quarter of a million tons of coal were purchased in advance. For the future the navy had only eight colliers, and no others were available from private American sources. Forty-one British ships along with other foreign vessels were chartered to deliver coal en route, a fleet more than twice as large, numerically, as the Battle Fleet itself—raising the justifiable

Theodore Roosevelt wanted to impress Americans and the world with a show of naval power

criticism that the proud, parading battleships were dependent on the outside world for fuel.

At the end of November the fleet assembled in New York, where Admiral Evans announced at a farewell banquet that his men were ready for "a feast, a frolic, or a fight." The following month the fleet arrived at Hampton Roads on schedule. There lighter after lighter moved from ship to shore delivering supplies: almost a million pounds of flour and a million pounds of fresh beef; hundreds of thousands of barrels of smoked ham and vegetables; forty thousand dozen eggs; and mammoth quantities of butter, bacon, raisins, pickles, cheese, bologna, nuts, and jams, and canned fruit and condensed milk. Not to be overlooked were fifteen thousand pounds of English plum pudding for Christmas, while the men themselves brought Christmas trees and holly wreaths from shore in preparation for the holidays.

During the week of waiting, sailors on leave played football on the grounds of Fort Munroe. Regattas were held among the crews. Those committed to shipbound duty spent endless hours in polishing the brass, the guns, the walnut decor of the bridges, and the golden shields and eagles of the ornate prows. Tons of white paint were lavished on the hulls and smokestacks, till the great ships glistened with a pristine glory. "In their immaculate white paint," the *Times* recorded, "they barely looked like the engines of destruction that they were."

At last the fateful day came. The enlisted forces of each ship lined up at quarters, where the division commander read to them the Articles of War. "Every man was told what his duty was to his country, to his flag, and to his superior officers." Aboard the *Mayflower* Admiral Evans made his farewells to the president. "One word before you go," said Roosevelt. "Your cruise is a peaceful one, but if it turns out otherwise you realize your responsibility." A peaceful cruise, yes, but one with frightening possibilities. It could, to one with overcharged imagination, make or break the image of America.

2
▶
Cool Welcome at Trinidad

▶
▶

It was precisely 10 A.M. A cold north wind etched lines of ragged whitecaps on the water. From the bridge of the *Mayflower,* President Roosevelt signaled Admiral Evans' flagship, the *Connecticut:* "Proceed upon duty assigned." Flags flashed the order down the line. The sixteen ships hove anchor, cables clattering through hawseholes, clouds of black smoke rising from the funnels. The *Connecticut* turned on its axis and the others followed to fall in line with the ease and precision of a drill squad. Sides gleaming in the sun, the column of white ships swerved towards Cape Henry, favored by the outgoing tide and the twenty-two-knot wind behind them.

For nine miles the *Mayflower* raced ahead, pausing to review the fleet at Horseshoe Shoals. "We wish you a pleasant journey," signaled Roosevelt, receiving Evans' curt reply of "Thank you." As each ship passed the presidential yacht, a twenty-one-gun salute exploded, puffs of smoke trailing aft and vanishing. Muffled in double-breasted overcoats, the sailors manned the rails and the admiral allowed their bottled-up emotions the relief of cheers. The president, "his jaws set, his expression serious," raised his silk hat in acknowledgment.

In exactly fifteen minutes the *Kentucky,* bringing up the rear, had cleared the entrance to the harbor, while the leading ship was almost over the horizon. The die had been cast. The Great White Fleet, for good or bad, was on its way.

Sky and sea were sparkling as the fleet sailed southeast for Trinidad, some eighteen hundred miles away. Two hours from Cape Henry, Admiral Evans broke the single file formation. It was too hard for him to keep track of the long, protracted line, and the vessels were bothered by one another's wake. He ordered the ships to form in parallel lines of four, extending over two square miles. Each foursome represented a division:

First Division	*Connecticut* (flagship)
	Kansas
	Louisana
	Vermont
Second Division	*Georgia* (flagship)
	Virginia
	New Jersey
	Rhode Island
Third Division	*Minnesota* (flagship)
	Ohio
	Missouri
	Maine
Fourth Division	*Alabama* (flagship)
	Illinois
	Kearsage
	Kentucky

There was a certain hierarchy in this order, the finest vessels in the vanguard and their weaker sisters to the rear. The new flagship *Connecticut,* pride of the navy, had cost $7,677,000 to build, displaced 16,000 tons, and had a maximum speed of 18 knots. (By way of comparison, although all battleships today are obsolete, the *Wisconsin* built in 1940 cost $110,000,000 and displaced 45,000 tons.) The little *Kentucky* had been built for half that cost in 1900, displaced only 11,500 tons, and had a maximum speed of 16.5 knots. Most of the ships were armored with four 12-inch guns, and from sixteen to twenty 6- to 8-inch guns. The smaller guns, designed for a day of wooden frigates when battles had been decided at close quarters, were virtually obsolete. The navy had intended to replace them but had never gotten to it.

For the first time in many weeks the fourteen thousand enlisted men aboard the fleet had time to take stock of their fate. "The talk aboard ship, before we left, was that we were going to war with Japan," wrote gunners mate Ambrose Jones of the *New Jersey,* though that war was more than thirty years away. There was a grim suggestion of this threat in the fact that all the Japanese stewards aboard the battleships had been discharged as potential spies, some having served loyally for twenty years or more. They had been replaced by Negro volunteers. (In grief at this injustice, one Japanese steward had earlier attempted suicide at the Brooklyn Navy Yard.)

That evening, sixty miles from Hatteras, the men received the true facts on their destination. Into the mess halls, by the new and magic wireless telegraphy, came Admiral Evans' message to his fleet:

The President authorizes the Commander-in-Chief to in-
form the officers and men that after a short stay on the Pa-
cific Coast it is the President's intention to have the fleet
return to the Atlantic Coast by way of the Mediterranean.

Around the world it was to be, an objective often hinted
at but not till now confirmed. Pride took possession of the
fleet. Theirs was to be a daring exploit that no other navy
in the world could match. And the rewards, from this safe
distance in the tranquil Gulf Stream, seemed immense.
Those who had yielded to the fresh-coined slogan of that
summer, "Join the navy and see the world!" looked forward,
starry-eyed, to the fulfillment of that promise.

Among the officers, however, there prevailed a quiet tension. To the world this cruise might seem a sort of jubilant
parade; to them it was a formidable challenge. Never before had such a venture been attempted. True, some battleships had sailed singly or in groups of two or three around
the globe. But the closest approximation to this cruise was
the voyage of the Russian Baltic Fleet around Cape Horn
(and partly through the Suez Canal) to the Sea of Japan
just two years earlier. Plagued by coaling problems, muti-
nies, and garbled navigation, the fleet had met complete disaster in Tsushima Strait, sunk or routed by the fresh guns of
the Japanese. Roosevelt had later told German Admiral
von Tirpitz that "there were fleets of the white race which
were totally different from the fleet of the poor [Russian
Admiral] Rozhestvenski." However, the grievous precedent
remained.

The enlisted men felt no such serious concern. Most of
them were still quite young—their average age was twenty-

Roosevelt wanted his navy manned by young and vigorous lads
—who would be willing to sacrifice their lives if need be

one—and they'd come from New England farms and fac-
tories and the plains states of the Middle West. To be at sea
was the adventure of a lifetime. Foreign observers won-
dered if this youthful navy would be up to fighting a full-
fledged war if such should be their fate. But Roosevelt himself had no such doubts. He wanted his navy manned by
young and vigorous lads in whom he had the greatest faith
—who'd be willing to sacrifice their lives if need be. "These
are the torch-bearers," he wrote of young men in the na-

tion's service. "These are they who have dared the Great Adventure."

It was not a bad life aboard ship and it quickly settled into comfortable routine, regulated by ninety-eight different bugle calls from the marines distributed about each ship. Reveille was at 5 A.M., followed by swabbing the decks and general clean-up until 7:15 breakfast. Drill call came at 9:30, with battleship drill continuing until 11:30. Dinner at noon, followed by shipboard duties until 4:30 when an hour and a half of leisure was allowed. Even this period saw little idleness. "There was plenty to keep you busy," wrote a boy on the *Virginia,* "washing hammocks and clothes, sewing, policing quarters and equipment."

There was plenty to do in the way of recreation, too. Among the tons of equipment brought aboard at Hampton Roads were 24 grand pianos, 60 phonographs, 300 sets of chess, 200 packs of playing cards, and equipment for handball, quoits, and billiards. For mere self-indulgence, 200,000 cigars were provided, 400,000 cigarettes, and 15,-000 pounds of candy. Each ship had its library, its collapsible stage for amateur theatricals, sheet music for group singing, nickelodeon peep shows (censored before leaving) in the lounges, ice cream and soft drinks at the ship's canteen. No liquor or "grog" had been served the navy since the Civil War, though officers were permitted beer and wine.

Much of the sailors' social life centered around the mess hall, as that of the officers did around the wardroom mess. The food ranged from good to excellent, and probably better for the sailors than for officers—since the latter had to purchase their own victuals. Wrote the fleet correspondent for *Harper's Weekly:* "The general impression of many has been that our sailors' fare has consisted of salt pork, beans, hardtack, coffee, and a few other articles, but if they were to see the menu of the ships of today they would be pleasantly surprised." He then went on to point out that "nearly everything one can think of to eat or drink is included in the ships' supplies," and listed such dishes as roast beef, veal fricassee, pork chops, pot pie, corned beef, rice and tapioca puddings, and jams and jellies for the galley-baked bread.

As they moved south into warmer climates, the bluejackets changed into their tropical white uniforms. Cleanliness and good personal appearance were enforced. Men washed their own garments during morning watches. Recruits were drilled in the use of the newfangled toothbrush. Showers had been installed aboard but linked directly to the boilers so that the water came out steaming hot, and the men resorted to the traditional procedure of bathing from buckets. Woe to the man who did not come out pristine clean. Captain H. C. Davis of the *Ohio* recalls the picture of "a big husky sergeant, with sand and canvas, scrubbing a recruit until he was as pink as the proverbial baby."

Cleanliness, however, came hard for the "Black Gang" of stokers in the boiler rooms, committed to keeping the hungry furnaces supplied with coal. Theirs was the sorriest role aboard the fleet, confined to the bowels of the ships where the temperatures soared to over a hundred and where the slogan of "join the navy and see the world" was mockery. Pale from the nature of their occupation, constantly grimy from embedded coal dust, they were often discriminated against when shore leave was provided, due to Roosevelt's edict that all men appearing in public must be "ruddy cheeked." Sickness was rife among the engine-room crews, and twenty-two cases of insanity were chalked up in the first two months.

Beyond this exceptional circumstance, illness aboard ship was no more than it would have been with any land-bound group, and even the farm boys from the Middle West were quick to get their sea legs. Two ships, the *Illinois* and the *Missouri,* were permitted to leave the fleet briefly on its course through the Caribbean, to take ill seamen to nearby shores for treatment. On December 22 the first death was reported, that of a sailor on the *Alabama* who succumbed to spinal meningitis. The fleet was stopped and appropriate sea burial observed.

Cruising steadily on a southeast course towards Trinidad, Evans drilled his ships in intricate maneuvers and formations. The average speed was ten knots, and the distance between ships an absolute 400 yards. The single file formation, stem to stern, was used principally in entering and leaving harbors. Otherwise, Evans preferred a "line of squadrons, natural order"—in which they marched in lines of four—or "column formation, open order," in which they proceeded in squares or diamonds in order of divisions.

To keep these hulking battlewagons in precise place, in an even moderately rough sea and commanding tides and winds, was a matter of considerable skill. It was like driving a car on a four-lane thruway and obeying all the traffic rules —one had to keep a lookout for the other fellow. "I was signalman on the *New Jersey*," wrote Anthony C. Miccia to the author, "and so far as I know we were never given a compass course except to follow orders from the flagship. We had quite a hard time maintaining course and position, as distance was 400 yards between the mainmast of the ship ahead and our forward bridge. Because of this close gap, the officers on the bridge were constantly telegraphing to the engineroom for one to four revolutions more or less, until they got over being squeamish."

Communication between ships, while still maintained to some extent by semaphore and signal flags, was principally by wireless telegraphy and telephone—the fleet being the first to make large-scale use of this new device at sea. In the case of the telephone, one veteran wrote, "The method employed was to shout into the instrument with a small megaphone." Martin Witmyer, chief electrician on the *Alabama,* claimed a world's record for sending his voice a distance of 1,100 miles. Ship to shore communication was by wireless telegraphy, the telephone not generally being as reliable as Witmyer had found it. "Think of it!" John Scott Merriweather wired *Harper's Weekly.* "Here we are, far out at sea, and yet able to send messages to New York! It is difficult to get quite used to this sort of thing."

Aboard the battleship *Louisiana,* in the First Division, was a dapper man dressed in white suit, straw hat, and silver-headed walking stick, who peered into everything— from the ship stores to the navigation instruments on the bridge. He was Franklin Matthews, reporter for "the world's greatest newspaper" the New York *Sun.* Matthews was one of a group of correspondents traveling with the fleet, all of whom were hand-picked and subject to the strictest censorship. No dispatch alien to the purpose of the cruise, or reflecting any unfavorable aspect of its operation, was allowed to pass the critical review of navy officers.

Matthews, among others, had been personally picked by Roosevelt who admired his Horatio Alger style. The president had also chosen artist Henry Reuterdahl, one of America's leading maritime painters, to record the voyage on canvas. The choice of Reuterdahl was less auspicious. Unknown to the president, he had contracted with *McClure's Magazine* for a series of articles on the fleet, and during its wait at Hampton Roads had circulated among the battleships and discovered many things amiss: to wit, that the vessels were lying too low in the water, submerging the armor belts that should have been above the water line. Both turret guns and broadside guns were positioned "far too low" and could not be fired in a pitching sea. Open ammunition shafts were too close to the guns; sparks from the latter might set fire to the magazines. Furthermore, he observed "that the vessels are unprovided with torpedoes and torpedo tubes and that the bureaucracy of the navy makes it impossible to improve these defects." He noted, too, along with cracked boiler tubes on certain vessels, that the *Kearsage* flaunted only wood and canvas armor plates in place of steel.

All this came out in the January issue of *McClure's,* shortly after the fleet's departure. The yellow press was quick to seize on the exposure with such headlines as "Battleship Fleet Fatally Defective." Congress was up in arms, demanding the immediate dismissal of the guilty correspondent. But it was many days before the culprit was identified, and meanwhile Reuterdahl continued with the fleet as an unsuspected, much respected painter.

On December 23 the coast of Venezuela was sighted, and at sundown Trinidad came into view. This was the moment of truth, the first confrontation with the crowds of British subjects who would greet the fleet with awe and admiration. The occasion took on an added significance because of the natural naval competition between England and the United States, and because Trinidad was one of Britain's most important stations in the Caribbean. As they coursed through the Dragon's Mouth into the Gulf of Paria and approached the island, the battleships reverted to single file and steamed ahead at eleven knots, maneuvering to neat alignment in the harbor and all dropping anchors simultaneously in a flawless exhibition of good seamanship.

Next morning the sun shown bright on the sleepy harbor town of Port of Spain. But where were the expected crowds, the brass bands, flags, and decorations, the excitement? The crews had been told that they would be warmly welcomed at Trinidad, but they could see only a few scattered Negroes on the docks, going unconcerned about their work. Regardless, two thousand recruits were picked for shore leave, and to guarantee their faultless behavior a new department of the navy had been organized, the shore patrol, among whose duties was to apprehend "any men who show the slightest trace of disorderly conduct."

Admiral Evans had expected the appropriate salutes from land batteries and a prompt visit to his flagship by the governor-general, Sir Henry Jackson. No such visit was forthcoming, and Evans went ashore to call on the governor

himself. (Anxious to save face with his readers, the san-
guine Franklin Matthews reported to the New York *Sun:*
"A journey of five miles out to the ship in the blazing sun,
Admiral Evans thought would be too much for him and
the Governor appreciated thoroughly the Admiral's solici-
tude for his health.") An uncensored photograph published
in *Harper's Weekly* for January 4 shows the admiral and
his staff "landing at Trinidad for the official call on the
Governor" and reveals not a single native or British official
in attendance. Port of Spain had closed its doors and
drawn its windowshades. Disgruntled officers attributed
this disregard to Race Week, an annual regatta on the
island, and the coming Christmas holidays. The fact was
that London, sensitive to relations with Japan, had advised
its British subjects to ignore "the American tramps" and
their presumptuous appearance. Accordingly, all the traditional Christmas balls, all normal festivities on the island
had been cancelled.

How would this look to the Americans back home, who
devoured news of the fleet like children after candy? Aware
of their responsibilities, reporters sent back stories of the
jubilant reception showered on the battleships at Trinidad
with "crowds on the waterfront, voicing their admiration."
"Sir Henry Jackson, the British Governor," said one dispatch, "was early aboard Admiral Evans' flagship." Wrote
the correspondent for the *New York Times:* "Two thousand men of Admiral Evans' battleship fleet got shore
leave this afternoon, and were warmly welcomed when they
landed. . . . The town presents a lively appearance, and
committees are looking after the sailors and officers."

Despite little evidence of welcome except from the local

police who were watchful and wary of their conduct, the men were eager to get ashore. Midshipman of the *Rhode Island,* Clifford Bemus, now a veteran of the cruise, recalls that one man who had been denied leave donned a life preserver, dove overboard, and started swimming toward the town. He had gone quite a distance when he was picked up by the ship's launch and returned to his vessel where "I guess he got the brig for stealing Government property and leaving the ship without permission."

There was little to entertain the men in Port of Spain beyond "biograph whiskey," so named because it projected its own motion pictures in the mind, and this was shunned by all but a reckless few. The town itself, reported chief turret captain Roman Miller "is interesting in a way, but not a fit place for Americans to live in." The sailors were puzzled by the lack of any warm reception, but were delighted with the fresh tropical fruit they were able to buy— a winter treat not available in the United States in 1907. They roamed the bazaars, being royally fleeced by native vendors, and loading up, in addition to straw hats, on parrots, parakeets, and monkeys. These latter were smuggled aboard the ships and camouflaged with deck paint to avoid detection. Gunners mate Jones concealed his parakeet in the armory and fed it dumplings dipped in coffee. "He was awfully hot in there," Jones remembered. "He would never say a word."

The cool reception from the town was somewhat offset aboard ship by the approaching Christmas holiday. Many recruits had been given permission to go ashore and amass greenery for decorations, returning with boatloads of palm fronds, bamboo leaves, and green vines with which the battleships, on Christmas eve, were decked from stem to stern. That evening boatloads of volunteer carolers took to the phosphorescent waters to serenade the floating castles with "Good King Wenceslaus" and "We Three Kings." It was open night to officers and ensigns (then known as "passed midshipmen") in the wardrooms of the fleet.

Christmas day itself was given over to athletic competitions—boxing, wrestling, boat races between crews—followed by a typical New England dinner of roast ham and turkey, cranberry sauce and candied yams, mince pie and plum pudding. The bandmasters led the men in singing carols; and Santa Claus made his traditional appearance on each vessel, dispensing gifts and favors. When Captain Wainwright of the *Louisiana* received a tin whistle, he obligingly tooted a tune for his appreciative men. Altogether, though several thousand miles from home, with the temperature ninety in the shade, the battleships succumbed completely to the Christmas spirit.

For the next few days the fleet was occupied with coaling, the most arduous duty of the cruise, and one that took place approximately every two weeks. All hands were obliged to take part in the task, working in half-hour shifts. Lighters were brought alongside, into which ashes from the furnaces were emptied. Then the colliers took the lighters' places, and 800-pound burlap bags were filled with coal and hoisted by derrick to the deck, to be poured down the chutes into the bunkers, there to be stowed evenly by the engine-room crews. It was sweaty, backbreaking work, and clouds of coal dust enveloped the snow-white ships and turned them gray in what, to Franklin Matthews' eyes, seemed "almost a profanation."

Yet Matthews, aware of the censors, saw the bright side of this hateful task. He informed his readers back home: "It was lively work, step and go, and laughter and good cheer enlivened the task. The ship's band was placed on the after bridge, where it played quicksteps and jigs and made the men run and heave and shovel and toss as if coaling ships was the greatest fun in the world."

Aboard the *Ohio* a coal passer in the bunkers saw a curious looking object. On inspection it proved to be half a stick of dynamite wrapped in waxed paper to keep it dry. He quickly took it to the captain who, unwilling to use the wireless to broadcast the dread discovery, had it sent by special courier to Evans. Evans was quick to see the implication. The possibilities of sabotage had haunted the division commanders from the beginning of the cruise. A few sticks of dynamite, carried aboard by seemingly innocent visitors, could seal the doom of half the American navy. There had been such incidents in other battleship parades abroad. The French battleship *Jena* had been blown up by a hidden stick of dynamite.

Instantly Evans added another order to the engine crews. Every delivery of coal, before it was shoveled in the furnaces, was to be combed by hand for any possible explosives. And visitors henceforth were to be barred from engine rooms—an order almost impossible to observe for reasons of diplomatic courtesy. Meanwhile, where was the other half of the piece of dynamite that they had found? For the next few weeks the ships' commanders were plagued with the nightmare of its reaching the *Ohio*'s furnaces. Months later it was determined that the uncovered stick of dynamite was typical of a type used in the coal mines of Virginia and might have accidentally come from that source.

Coaling was finished on the afternoon of December 29, and almost immediately the sixteen battleships weighed anchor, anxious to be clear of Trinidad. Perhaps that inhospitable island had suffered pangs of conscience, for at the last minute Governor Jackson, setting aside London's orders to ignore the fleet, sent a note to Amiral Evans which read in part: "Congratulations on the irreproachable behavior of your men on leave. . . . I can assure you that your men established a record hard to equal and impossible to beat." Copies of the note were posted in the wardrooms of all ships.

Trinidad's coolness and indifference towards the fleet was admitted even by the Pollyanna-minded Matthews ("Let the truth be known! Trinidad didn't warm up to the fleet at al!"), and was reported more analytically by correspondent Robert Dunn who was later removed from the cruise by Roosevelt for his frank opinions. Dunn wrote on January 25 that the arrival of the fleet at Port of Spain "has made less ripple on the surface life of this metropolis than a band of tourists on a 63-day cruise."

Dunn went on to reveal what was probably the real reason for this diffidence: "You see, only lately the *Dreadnought* took a practice run over here (at seventeen knots average speed, by the way) and the British Colonial, who likes his lion roaring so loud he must put cotton in his ears, respects a Yankee fleet no more than a squadron of tramps and luggers."

Indeed, something of a shadow had been thrown upon the fleet's expedition by the commissioning, a year before, of Great Britain's *Dreadnought* which made even the *Connecticut* seem behind the times. Nearly 500 feet long, with 17,900 tons displacement, she was by far the largest battleship yet launched. Not only that, she mounted ten 12-inch guns to, for example, the *Connecticut*'s two, and rejected entirely the 6-inch guns so prevalent on American ships but useless in all but close-in fighting. The *Dreadnought* had a maximum speed of 21 knots, and one third of her fuel consisted of oil, presaging the end of coal-dependent battleships.

Now it was learned that six other battleships of the *Dreadnought* class had been laid down, and the bitter fact was, to those who would face it, that the vessels of the Great White Fleet were close to obsolete. While the fleet remained a formidable fighting force, unsurpassed by any navy save Great Britain's, it was plain that the future lay in *Dreadnought*-class ships and, measured against time, the vessels of the Great White Fleet were doomed. There were Anglophobes in America who believed that Great Britain had timed the launching of the *Dreadnought* to deliberately diminish the propaganda value of the cruise. This would seem unlikely. *Dreadnought* had been under consideration since 1905, when Russia's naval defeat by the Japanese at Tsushima had indicated the need for greater speed and a greater number of long-range guns.

For that matter, even before the Great White Fleet set

sail the United States too was laying plans for dreadnoughts of her own. In May of 1907, Congress had authorized construction of two 20,000-ton battleships, each more formidable than Britain's *Dreadnought,* with twelve 12-inch guns and a top speed of 21 knots—to be completed by 1910. On commission or building were eight other first-class battlewagons. If the cruise of the Great White Fleet accomplished nothing more, it would have launched a race for bigger and better battleships involving every major nation of the world, as well as many minor countries infected by the fever.

3

▶

Rolling Down to Rio

▶
▶

So it was through the Serpent's Mouth and off to Rio de Janeiro, three thousand miles southeast of Trinidad. Ahead of them lay one of the longest legs of the cruise, in which the ships were forced to buck an adverse Amazon current carrying with it mighty swells that lifted the iron monsters like twigs and dropped them shudderingly into the troughs. The torpedo flotilla had preceded them, as it did on the first leg of the voyage, and only the supply ships and the *Yankton* were their escorts.

Where previously they had averaged ten or eleven knots in the smooth Caribbean, the ships were now held to nine knots by the current, and Admiral Evans chafed at the delay. He was due in Rio on January 10, and the efficiency of his operation would be measured in Washington partly by his adhesion to schedule. Yet there was the ever-present worry of coal consumption. At all costs the shame of towing a battleship into port must be avoided. In spite of the need for speed, orders went down the line for every vessel to conserve fuel, an order directed particularly at the Fourth Division and the *Maine,* which had proved to be such a glutton that extra bags of coal were carried on her decks. Competition in coal conservation was established between the ships, and at noon each day the flags went up to tell how much coal had been used and how much each ship had on hand.

Anthony C. Miccia, the White Fleet veteran, wrote: "Under way from Trindad to Rio the *New Jersey* shocked the Admiral with our noon coal report. Instead of consuming 95 to 96 tons per day, our consumption shot up to 135 tons. With a capacity of 1,800-odd tons it was easy to figure what would happen if we struck heavy weather for a few days. One trouble was, we discovered that the coal taken on at Trinidad had a high dirt content. We received a signal from Flag that the *Kansas* would take us in tow if we were not able to reach Rio.

"You cannot imagine the effect of this message on the whole crew. We would have been unable to live it down if we were towed in. Among the signalmen of the fleet it was a source of amusement to send us messages when things were slack. These went as follows: 'We are making a collection of spare coal. Send over for it.' Or 'We have picked over our ashes and have collected a few bags of coal. Please send boat.' 'Why don't you hoist your forecastle and quarter-deck awnings and sail into Rio?'

"It was a close call but we arrived in Rio with 21 tons of coal in our bunkers, above five normal hours of steaming."

Signalman Miccia also remembered: "It was on this leg of our journey that I learned to stay awake on the mid watch. In those days we did not get coffee at night and about 3 A.M. it was difficult to keep awake. No walking back and forth at sea as the captain slept in his sea cabin located on the lower bridge. An old-time quartermaster told me to stand up close to the bridge rails, rest my chin on the top rail, and if I fell asleep my knees would buckle and I'd receive a sharp rap on the chin. This was a drastic measure, but so was the punishment for sleeping on watch. It was rugged treatment but very effective."

New Year's Eve provided a raucous break in the increasing tedium. Officers assembled in the wardrooms early in the evening to drink toasts and sing appropriate songs. But the spirit of the occasion quickly got out of hand. Bands of ensigns dressed as Indians and pirates routed their shipmates from the hammocks, and with drums and whistles all but took possession of the ships. Contrary to regulations, the sirens were sounded—ordinarily a signal of distress at sea—searchlights were commandeered to sweep the skies, New Year's wishes passed between the ships by semaphore, and even the engine-room furnace doors were plastered with the message, Happy New Year!

In the face of this mutinous behavior, captains remained discreetly in their rooms. Even Admiral Evans had come to accept the edict that the vessels under his command must be run as "happy ships," and that the boisterous spirits of his men should not be crushed. He knew that the propaganda value, to naval recruitment, of letters written home and news dispatches of such revelry aboard, was of incalculable worth. When quarters were sounded at nine next morning, there was no suggestion of rebuke to the now chastened ranks that assembled for the day.

As they rounded the bulge of Brazil, three incidents both amusing and disturbing broke the tedium. On January 2 a man on the *Illinois* reported seeing a life raft to the west, with two men clinging to it. Unwilling to break line to send a battleship to the rescue, Evans ordered the escort *Culgoa* to investigate. The *Culgoa* was back in two hours with the report that the life raft had proved to be a Brazilian catamaran with two fishermen aboard. The latter had been duly flattered by this attention from a man of war, but a little miffed that the well-meaning *Culgoa* had disturbed their fishing waters.

Two days later, at 2:30 in the morning, the *Missouri's* guns boomed, signaling "man overboard." Evans ordered the entire fleet stopped while boats were lowered from the *Missouri, Illinois,* and *Kearsage.* In the rays of searchlights the boats were rowed in a criss-cross pattern covering the area for half an hour, when hope was given up for finding the lost sailor. The unfortunate seaman must have been killed while falling or caught in the churn of the propeller. Later, checking her crew as the fleet proceeded, the *Missouri* sheepishly reported that she *thought* that a man had fallen overboard, but it seemed that a sailor had had a nightmare and shouted the warning in his sleep.

A more alarming incident occurred the following evening while the ships were cruising in formation at 400 yards apart. A watchman aboard the *Louisiana* sighted a strange-looking object headed towards them on a collision course. It proved to be a barkentine with no lights and no apparent helmsman. The attack alarm was sounded and marines grabbed their rifles as the vessel barely missed the *Louisiana,* changed her course, and bore down on the *Georgia.*

Just in time the *Georgia* sheered off from the vessel's path causing the Second Division to use similar evasive tactics. Then, as swiftly as it appeared, the mysterious Flying Dutchman sailed into the night. Who was she, sailing without lights and seemingly without a helmsman? Some vessel sent by the Japanese to disrupt the fleet, possibly loaded with explosives? How was she able to wend her way through an entire fleet of cruising battleships? The mystery was never solved, but it gave rise to thoughts of how vulnerable the battlewagons were to unpredictable encounters.

As they approached the equator, preparations began for the traditional initiation ceremonies, by which every man who had not yet "crossed the line" received the official but sometimes dreaded welcome of King Neptune. Apprehensive neophytes aboard the ships were allowed to overhear such remarks as, "What was the name of that coal passer they killed on the *Wheeling* on Neptune Day?" This time King Neptune warned each ship of his impending arrival by telephone.

As Neptune arrived, took over command from the ship's captain and mounted his throne between the forward turrets, those who had not yet crossed the line—two thirds of the fleet's complement—were brought forth for the hazing that for years had been a navy ritual. Eddie Holland, the *Virginia's* drummer, recently recalled from memory his experience. "They grabbed me, made me sign the log, and whacked me as I bent over. 'Dr. Pill' handed me a huge chunk of dough, loaded with red pepper, and said 'Swallow.' Then the barber lathered me with a paint brush and swiped it off with a hockey-stick 'razor.' Right then, there was a push and I flopped backwards into a canvas tank, half drowned!"

Not even officers, mascots, or reporters were immune, although Holland recalled, "You know, an officer could buy his way out of that ceremony—if he could dig up six bottles of beer for Neptune's party." Following the hazing, each of the bedraggled victims was presented with a certificate announcing his acceptance into Neptune's kingdom as a "trusty shellback." Of all souvenirs the men were to return with, this bit of parchment was perhaps the most revered.

Below the equator, the men sweated in nothing but their shorts. In extreme heat, navy discipline relaxed regarding dress. But not on all occasions. Matthews recalled the sailors listening to a band concert in the lounge. The performance closed, appropriately, with the playing of "The Star-Spangled Banner" for which the audience rose. At this point, an officer demanded that all men don their uniforms. Nobody could stand for the national anthem in his underwear!

They were now approaching Rio, and two days behind their schedule (needless to say the ships had neither stopped nor slowed for the initiation ceremonies). Evans pressed his fleet for maximum speed, but there were inevitable breakdowns in equipment. Those shamed by such interruptions were sent to the "observation ward," or positioned between the two columns of ships, well to the rear. The *Maine* was a frequent occupant of this position, and the Admiral threatened to tow her into Rio if her officers did not improve her operation.

Evans was already showing signs of strain. He suffered grievously from rheumatic gout, and had already passed the age of strenuous duty. Second in command was Rear Admiral Thomas of the Third Division, followed by Rear

Admiral Sperry of the Fourth Division. These men too were close to sixty, and the average age of battleship captains was fifty-six, far higher than those in the other navies of the world. Seniority was in a sense determined not by fitness but by length of service.

There was another troublesome matter concerning Evans. Though commander of one of the greatest battle fleets afloat, he had not been granted the rank of full-scale admiral. This was due to a whim of Congress which, after granting a five-star admiral's rank to Dewey for his victory over the Spanish at Manila, had decided that such exalted titles were not in keeping with democracy. Henceforth only the two-star rank of rear admiral would be awarded fleet commanders. But how would this look to officials in Brazil, and to other South American countries where exalted naval titles were a dime a dozen? Evans and all his brother officers would be outranked and possibly humiliated by official protocol.

As far back as November the New York Times had called attention to this gross discrepancy. "The incongruity of having so vast a force under the command of an officer with no higher rank than that of Rear-Admiral is recognized everywhere except in Congress. The creation of the rank of Vice-Admiral and bestowing it on 'Fighting Bob' would, of course, not increase the competence of that distinguished officer; but the rank would be a more fitting one for the commander-in-chief of this mighty fleet." Nothing had come from this or other admonitions.

On top of these irritants, the fleet had lost its screen of six torpedo boats. These had put in for minor repairs at the

Brazilian port of Pernambuco. Here the crews had tangled with belligerent natives, and twenty-one men had been committed to the local jail with no date set for their release. While the loss of the torpedo escorts hardly put the battleships in jeopardy, the fleet felt strangely naked in their absence. And again, how would this absence look to the officials in Brazil as well as the authorities in Washington?

If there had been doubts about the fleet's reception by its South American host, raised by the bitter pill of Trinidad, these were quickly put to rest. Seventy-five miles east of Rio the telegraphed message was received, "Welcome American Fleet"; and twelve miles from the harbor they were greeted by three Brazilian warships headed out to greet them. Significantly, the Brazilian vessels fired a thirteen-gun salute, the salute befitting a vice-admiral, ignoring Congress' failure to accord this rank to Evans.

As they sailed in single column into Batafoga Bay, city and harbor burst their seams in welcome. The water was alive with boats—tugs, steamers, pleasure craft of all description flying flags and bunting. Crowds lined the waterfront, and the hills behind were black with spectators, thousands of whom, it was later learned, had waited and held their places two days for the fleet's arrival. Whistles shrieked, and warships thundered in salute. It sounded, wrote Franklin Matthews, like the Battle of Trafalgar.

Among the throng of warships in the harbor was the German cruiser *Bremen,* dispatched by the kaiser to keep tabs on the fleet, and the only foreign vessel in the harbor. Twice on the way from Trinidad, German warships had opportunely crossed paths with the American Great White

Fleet and signaled their respects. It was as if the German navy had elected quietly to keep track of the fleet's movements, share by proxy in its ceremonial receptions, and promote the kaiser's goal of German-American naval solidarity.

That night the sixteen battleships were strung from stem to stern with green and yellow lights in honor of Brazil. Their hosts responded with fireworks from the surrounding hills, and searchlights from Brazilian cruisers traced their patterns in the skies. Though it was too late for men or officers to go ashore, few in Rio or aboard ship got much sleep on that illuminated night, and Franklin Matthews happily recorded in his notes, "The Americans took Rio by storm."

They took Rio by storm in a less auspicious way, too. On the following day, when selected hundreds of "reliable" men were granted shore leaves, two innocent sailors strayed into a small cafe. In a fight among Brazilian patrons, one of the sailors was struck by a flying bottle. He promptly attacked the offender, who fled to the street and rounded up supporters. The free-for-all which followed was joined by scores of crewmen and hundreds of Brazilians. The local police were called, and picked up rocks to side with the civilians. Whereupon the cavalry was summoned to the Americans' support, and charged the police with flying sabres. As fast as the fighting was quelled in one part of the city it exploded in another.

The fray had inevitable consequences. Shore leaves were immediately cancelled. Reporters with the fleet were cautioned to make no mention of the incident. Admiral Evans told the press: "The occurrence was only a drunken row,

which was quickly stopped by the local police and the pa-
trols from the ships." To indicate his confidence in future
law and order, he announced that 4,000 men would go
ashore the following day. The Brazilian government sent
apologies, and Rio newspapers were urged to display, in
English, such headlines as "Hail the American Eagle!"

Matthews reduced the fracas to a single paragraph for
home consumption: a worthy Yankee had been accosted
by a razor-wielding bully and had flattened him with "a
good American right to the jaw." *Harper's Weekly* took occasion to editorialize: "The American blue-jacket is a sober,
ambitious young fellow with abundant self-respect and excellent taste in the amusement he seeks." That settled the
matter. Brazilian Foreign Minister Branco also publicly
praised the "culture, courtesy, and manners" of the Yankee
seamen.

Despite this mayhem—or perhaps because of it, con-
sidering the Latin temperament—the fleet's visit was a bril-
lant triumph. Relations remained warmly cordial through
the next ten days and hordes of two thousand to five
thousand men were granted shore leave, with no unpleasant
outbreaks. Rio de Janeiroans had gone to great lengths to
make the sailors feel at home. The streets were decked
with crossed American and Brazilian flags; information
booths were posted at strategic corners; twenty thousand
guides and maps were distributed to the visitors in uniform. For one milreis, or about thirty cents, sailors could
save themselves the trouble of writing home by purchasing
a typewritten letter which described their reception in Rio
and the sights they had witnessed in the city.

And, generally well behaved, the sailors took possession

of the city. They patronized the cinemas and nickelodeons (this time uncensored), piled on the trams and toured the streets in cabs, rode by funicular railway to the top of Mount Cordova, and learned to drink limeade in place of the strong Brazilian coffee. Only one deviation from this pattern could have led to trouble. Two hotly opposed political parties had organized parades, and both sides urged the jolly sailors to participate. Sensing danger, the MPs hauled the Americans from the ranks before the lines of marchers clashed in battle.

On the officers' level, Admiral Evans missed the lavish ceremonies planned ashore. His gout was worse, and his physical condition poor. While he retained command, his duties were turned over to Admiral Thomas, of the Third Division, who suffered from a weak heart. Thomas carried on as best he could, though the round of official breakfasts, lunches, and dinners took their toll of all the officers. Innumerable toasts had been drunk in courtesy, and the forced consumption of alcohol imperiled many officers' careers. Meanwhile, Evans remained in his cabin, and singularly enough, his only visitor was the German captain of the *Bremen* who seemed to feel that he was somehow host by proxy to the fleet.

Brazil's enthusiasm for the fleet had one embarrassing angle. The recently elected president, Alfonse Penna, saw in the visit a tribute to his pro-American administration, a sign that Americans recognized Brazil as the leading nation among South American republics. Naval minded, he had ordered the delivery of several battleships from English shipyards to justify this proud position. Now he spoke slyly of a forthcoming alliance between Brazil and the United

States, and Rio papers jumped at the suggestion, one boldly stating that such a treaty had been signed by the United States.

Before Washington could jump to a denial, another more foreboding matter occupied the fleet. Once again the rumor-mongers began spreading trouble. Stories were rife of plans to sabotage the fleet. Warnings were spread of dynamite smuggled into bunkers, of frogmen seen planting mines beneath the ships, of Japanese guns perched on the hills to shell the battleships. From Paris came reports that German agents were plotting to dynamite the fleet to precipitate war between Japan and the United States and bring about a German-American alliance.

These rumors reached such a pitch that American sailors on shore leave learned to their alarm that the *Connecticut* had been blown up in the harbor. Hurrying to the shore, they saw the flagship floating calmly at its mooring. But the report was relayed home and irresponsibly circulated, causing the Japanese ambassador to demand immediate retraction of any charges concerning his country's aims against the fleet.

While the Brazilian government had taken all security precautions, and patrolled the harbor nightly, the city's police were haunted by the rumored plots. There seemed to be only one solution—find a scapegoat and dispose of him. This they did, reporting a single anarchist named Fedher had been found responsible for all the intrigue and conniving. They had driven him into the jungle where "he has doubtless been eaten by wild animals."

A less publicized bit of intrigue was the disappearance of five sailors who had started home as stowaways aboard the liner *Byron*. They were discovered some days later, while the vessel was at sea, by its 200-pound chief officer who had stepped on the matting beneath which they were hiding. Queried as to their motives for deserting, they said simply, "We got tired of the navy."

On their last full day in Rio, January 21, a reception for Brazilian high officials was held aboard the *Minnesota*. Henry Reutedahl, again in charge of decorations, had decked the battleship with greenery and turned the forward deck into a bower of potted plants, rock gardens, waterfalls and goldfish-laden pools. Three thousand guests from shore attended, conspicuous among them being a group of German officers from the *Bremen*. The ship's band struggled bravely with the intricate bars of the Brazilian national anthem, which the musicians found "queer music; it goes hippety hop." While only soft drinks could be served on deck, Admiral Thomas took President Penna and Foreign Minister Branco to his cabin to sample his vintage wine and champagne.

The following afternoon the ships weighed anchor and steamed seaward, accompanied, as an act of courtesy, by sixteen Brazilian cruisers. As they left the harbor, fog descended and raised havoc with their orderly departure. Thirty-two warships groped in helpless apprehension, signaling and whistling at each other in a desperate effort to avoid collision. As they reached the open sea, the fog bank mercifully lifted and with final salutes the Great White Fleet steamed free of its escorting hosts and headed south towards Tierra del Fuego.

4

►

The Challenge of the Straits

►
►

It was not Roosevelt's intention, in his concept of the fleet's voyage, to pay any signal honors to the Latin American republics. They were unimportant to him, far secondary to Japan and European nations which needed to be impressed with United States naval power. South America was simply a geographical obstruction to be circumnavigated on the way to the Pacific. Calls were scheduled only for Brazil and Peru, with coaling stops at Chile's Punta Arenas and Magdalena Bay in Mexico.

But this matter of visits had become a Frankenstein blown up out of all proportions, particularly following the honors shown Brazil and her tumultuous and publicized response. Now eleven Latin American republics, including even tiny Uruguay, demanded similar recognition from the fleet. High on this list was Argentina, traditional rival of Brazil for hemispheric leadership. When, demanded the Argentine government, would the fleet appear at Buenos Aires to pay honor to their sovereign country? The American government, seeking a valid excuse, replied that the Río de la Plata was too shallow to accommodate the fleet. Well, then, how about a small detachment such as the torpedo boats? To this, Secretary of the Navy Metcalf agreed. The crews of the flotilla had been finally released from jail in Pernambuco, and the squadron was available. Admiral Evans protested hotly that his fleet would once again be without its escort, but to no avail, and on January 25 the six torpedo boats sped up the Plata.

The visit was brief, but Buenos Aires burst its seams in lavish welcome, striving to outdo the boisterous hospitality of Rio and all but smothering the small detachment of a hundred Yankee sailors. After this formality the torpedo boats raced down the Plata, passing the Uruguayan capital of Montevideo where, to everyone's surprise, vast crowds had assembled on the shoreline. Somehow Uruguay too had expected some attention from the fleet, and was highly miffed when the boats sped past and merely waved—causing Secretary of State Root to send his formal apologies to the Uruguayan government.

Moving south, the battleships now encountered heavy weather. The temperature dropped. The crews reverted from white uniforms to blue; jackets and sweaters were in order. Gales and rain, with waves as high as twenty-five feet, plagued the fleet. As visibility dropped, maintaining position by telephone or wireless proved unreliable. "And of course," wrote Anthony Miccia, signalman on the *New Jersey,* "visual signals were out. This meant trying to hold position by whistle sound, which was nerve racking with sixteen whistles blowing, and estimates of sound were very deceptive, as loudness of sound at sea does not always mean the sound is close. The hardest part is to locate the position and direction."

Apparently Argentina had not settled for the cursory visit from the six torpedo boats, or else had been inspired to prolong the ceremonies. By telegraph Evans learned that a squadron of Argentine warships was pursuing them, in hopes of making a rendezvous at sea. When he learned they were close, and approaching in a nighttime fog, he ordered the sixteen battleships to train their multiple flashlights on the skies, providing a beacon to establish their position. The courtesy was effective, and that night the two fleets joined and sailed together, side by side.

The following day presented an event unique in naval history. Battleship pageants held in inland seas or close to shore were commonplace throughout the world. Warships had passed each other on the high seas with appropriate courtesies. But never before had two fleets peacefully rendezvoused to honor each other far from shore. Now Argentine Admiral Olivo saluted Evans with a fifteen-gun salute, innocently raising him to the rank of admiral, and Evans replied with twenty-one guns blasting from all his sixteen battleships. The two fleets then paraded for each other's benefit; bands came on deck to play their respective national anthems; sailors manned the rails to cheer each other as they passed. "I never saw sentiment carried so far in all my naval experience," said one American officer. "Perhaps it was unusual, but it was impressive, it was impressive." The Buenos Aires *Herald* called it a Moment in History, "the first great naval pageant ever to take place on the high seas."

Aboard his Fourth Division flagship, *Alabama,* Admiral Sperry was impressed. He was impressed with the executions of the visiting fleet, "pretty good for a South American squadron," and more particularly with their war-green color. Sperry was third in the line of command, and took his responsibilities (as well as possibilities, for he was sure that Evans would some day have to be replaced) with weighty self-importance. He now wired Secretary Metcalf requesting that the Great White Fleet be painted gray; it would make them less conspicuous in case of an emergency. Metcalf, knowing Roosevelt's feelings on this matter, ordered that the ships remain what Sperry called "abominable white."

As the fleet approached the Straits of Magellan, the weather was what one expected from that region. "Only the cranks took a cold shower in the morning," Franklin Matthews noted. New stars appeared in storm-flecked skies, and the Southern Cross was sighted. On January 31 Cape Virgin's headland came into view and Admiral Thomas, still in command by proxy, ordered the fleet to anchor in Possession Bay till daybreak brought them sufficient light to navigate the straits.

Ahead of them lay the trickiest and by tradition the most potentially dangerous test of the fleet's entire voyage—the 350-mile passage through the straits. Occasionally single warships, even two or three together, had successfully made the passage, and these included the U.S.S. *Oregon* which had sailed alone from the Pacific during the Spanish-American War, its thirty-six guns becoming a decisive factor in the destruction of Cervera's fleet off Santiago. Never before, however, had sixteen battleships together, committed to keeping in close formation, undertaken such a challenge.

Recruits aboard the battleships were plied with legends

of the perils of the straits by those few veterans who had made the passage. There were the "willywaws," or satan-ridden winds that blasted vessels from the water. There were the cannibalistic Indians of Tierra del Fuego who, as the name "Land of Fire" signified, lit misleading flares on shore to lure ships to the rocks. There were sea serpents with an appetite for sailors, and whirlpools rivaling Poe's Maelstrom, capable of swallowing a vessel whole.

Rumors of threats against the fleet appeared more credit-able now. It was here if anywhere that an enemy would catch them at a disadvantage, unable to maneuver freely, trapped between sheer-rising cliffs. Claude H. Wetmore, a popular author of maritime stories, warned his readers that the straits had been mined, and urged the fleet to go around the Horn. Stories circulated that enemy torpedo boats lurked in the hidden fords and estuaries, that a fleet of Japanese submarines and warships waited in ambush at the western exit of the straits. They might be nothing more than ru-mors, but what if they were true?

It was indeed a fact that the Fuegian Indians often shifted lights and buoys in the channel to mislead ships and plunder any that were wrecked. And there was no myth in the tidal rips and currents that made navigation difficult, the great winds that stormed between the rocky walls, the thick fogs that descended from the glaciers. In the preceding twenty years, more than fifty ships had gone to the bottom in this "graveland of the deep."

The shorter, easier portion of the passage brought the fleet, unscathed, to Punta Arenas, the southernmost city in the world. Once established as a penal colony when Chile

The Passing of the Great White Fleet
through the Straits of Magellan.
Painted by Henry Reuterdahl in 1907

captured it from Spain, the Chilean authorities had left the city on its lawless own since 1877. Its 12,000 population, living in huts of corrugated iron, numbered former convicts, smugglers, fugitives and fortune hunters, with a smattering of miners, ranchers, and sheep herders who made tidy fortunes trading with the north. Since Punta Arenas was a free port, smuggling was a leading occupation. In fact, the secrecy of night was so important to this operation that the smugglers resented the fleet's searchlights which were often trained on shore.

Above all, Punta Arenas was a paradise for foreign agents spying on the east-west traffic through the straits. They made no secret of their missions and affected no disguises. Theirs was a recognized profession. One Russian spy, Alexis Diatchkoff, had followed the fleet by land from Rio, miffed that he had not been allowed aboard, and the Russians complained of the fleet's unfair discrimination— surely the spies of other nations had been granted access to the ships. Two Japanese who had also tracked the fleet now stood conspicuously on the cliffs, studying the warships with binoculars. A Chilean port captain told of "four mysterious Orientals" who had entered the town and "vanished like shadows" fifteen days before. The British cruiser *Sappho* had appeared from nowhere and anchored nearby with no apparent purpose other than to scrutinize the battleships.

The town itself, to the recruits who went ashore, seemed dreary and innocuous. Greeting them was a large sign painted on the sea wall, "Special Prices to Americans." It proved true. Prices had been doubled, particularly on the precious furs which were the city's chief commodity. Pic-

ture postcards from this jumping-off place of the world, to
send to friends and relatives back home, were so much in
demand that the local post office ran out of stamps and had
to shut down.

While the natives were cordial towards the fleet, and
stripped the city of policemen as a gesture of hospitality,
Punta Arenas was essentially a coaling stop, and much of
the visit was spent at work around the colliers. During this
time the fleet was joined by the torpedo boat flotilla which
had finally caught up from Buenos Aires. It was also joined
by the Chilean cruiser *Chacabuco* which had come from
Valparaiso to extend its welcome and to help as it could in
guiding the Americans through the remaining straits.

The *Chacabuco*'s arrival was marred by one unfortunate
incident. At a reception for fleet officers aboard the ship,
a belligerent marine from the *Louisiana* with too much
wine inside him knocked a Chilean officer to the floor. Difficult apologies were made and injured dignity appeased,
when the marine struck again. This time the offender was
overcome and hustled off the ship to be placed in irons in
the *Louisiana*'s brig. Fearful of the possible adverse pub-
licity, Admiral Evans sent formal apologies to the captain
of the *Chacabuco* which, to his infinite relief, were grac-
iously accepted.

Before daybreak, February 7, the fleet hoisted anchors
and proceeded warily through the worst part of the straits,
walled in by towering snow-capped cliffs, menaced by submerged rocks, blasted by willywaws that only barely failed
to live up to exaggerated legends. Intermittent fogs obscured the buoys, and leadsmen measured the approaching

depths like blind men tapping their immediate surround-
ings with a cane. No officer caught a wink of sleep throughout that seventeen-hour day. At the point where the Atlantic and Pacific tides met in foaming conflict, disputing
the unequal heights between the oceans, the giant battleships were momentarily jarred off course, but struggled
back into position. No human error marred their passage.
The *Vermont* slipped a cog in her steering gear and dropped briefly out of line, but that was all. By nightfall they
had come abeam of the Evangelistas Islands and "for the
first time in history American naval power was concen-
trated in the Pacific."

Once again, steaming up the western coast of South
America, Rear Admiral Evans was beset by problems of
battleship diplomacy. His next scheduled stop was Callao,
Peru, and then a coaling and target-practice break at
Magdalena Bay in Mexico. But Chile was not content with
the fleet's stopover at Punta Arenas, her least important
harbor. She demanded more attention. Like all Latin
American countries who had once regarded the United
States with apprehension, and its Monroe Doctrine as an
instrument of Yankee imperialism, she now envied the
naval might of her northern neighbor, and sought to emu-
late it. A visit from the fleet would not only arouse the
Chilean public to the glory of the battleship, but would
suggest a sort of naval bond with the United States.

The problem of according Chile further honors, such as
a stop at Valparaiso, was a ticklish one for Evans. Only
fifteen years before, when Chile was in a revolutionary
ferment, a group of American sailors on shore leave from
the U.S.S. *Baltimore,* had been attacked by a mob in Val-

paraiso. Several were killed and a number wounded. The United States protested this "inhuman and revolting brutality" and the two countries were brought to the brink of war. The matter was resolved when Evans, then captain of the *Yorktown,* had steamed into Valparaiso and threatened to "blow the city to hell" if redress and apology were not forthcoming. "This timely display of firmness . . . produced a change of heart in our opponents." Chile backed down and offered reparations.

Now Evans feared a repetition of the Chilean affair. And he hated to lose time with a stop at Valparaiso. A meeting of the respective navies on the high seas, such as that observed with Argentina, would have been a good solution, but the suggestion would have had to come from Chile. Evans decided on a compromise. He would not drop anchor in Valparaiso, but simply sweep through the harbor with appropriate salutes.

This happy idea was executed, after telegraphing Valparaiso of their coming. As the fleet approached, the shores and hills were thronged with people, and a sign on the terraced highlands spelled out "Welcome." The letters were formed by white-dressed Chilean sailors stretched out on the terrace. But the effect was lost, wrote chief turret captain Miller of the *Vermont,* when one man apparently responded to a call of nature and deserted his crucial position in the "W."

Led by the *Connecticut,* the line of battleships swerved at full speed into the crescent-shaped harbor sending up "beautiful clouds of foam." From the flagship came the signal "prepare to salute," and at once (wrote Franklin Matthews), *the sixteen battleships roared out a salvo such as no one in Chile had ever heard before. The effect of the thunder was electric. People on the shore were seen to jump and run. All along the shore line below Fort Valdivia they began to race back toward the city and harbor by the thousands. It was literally a stampede. Great clouds of dust engulfed them and partly hid them from view. It made those on the ships laugh.*

However, the crowds recovered from this innocent bombardment; bands on shore broke out with the "Star-Spangled Banner"; and batteries responded to the fleet's salutes. As the battleships came abeam of Chilean President Montt's awaiting yacht, each vessel fired twenty-one guns, then followed the line into the broad Pacific. Chile had indeed been honored, and the fleet had done itself proud. Chilean-American relations were secure. Evans at this point sent a message to his men:

The Commander-in-Chief thanks the officers and men of the fleet for the handsome way they did the trick today.

Evans was popular with the recruits. As Dallas D. Lore, U.S.N.R., wrote to the author: "I shall *always* remember how thoughtful Admiral Evans was regarding the enlisted personnel. He was a very strict disciplinarian, but always fair." But Evans' position was becoming increasingly equivocal. Since taking to his cabin with the gout at Rio de Janeiro, he had been an absentee commander, leaving Rear Admiral Thomas to assume his duties. Thomas had waded through the tiresome ceremonies at Rio and Punta Arenas; he had guided the fleet through the Straits of Magellan. There were officers who thought that, as second in command, he should place Evans on the compulsory sick list and assume command himself.

This, to his credit, Thomas would not do. When doubts about Evans came from Washington, Thomas told the press: "There has not been a day that Rear Admiral Evans has not had full grasp of the duties of supreme commander. It has been my great pleasure to represent him socially from time to time. . . ."

But others were not so kind. In the chain of command following Evans were, in order of seniority, Rear Admiral Charles D. Sperry commanding the Fourth Division on the flagship *Alabama,* and William P. Emory commanding the Second Division on the flagship *Georgia.* Of the two, by far the more ambitious was Sperry, who bombarded authorities in Washington with written innuendos aimed at his personal promotion. Sperry wrote his wife of a letter he had sent to Secretary of the Navy Metcalf: "I also told him privately Evans was very ill and must give up, which would precipitate the question of Commander-in-Chief. Of course, in my letter to the secretary I said absolutely nothing of my aspirations."

While it was plain to many that, as Sperry added to his wife, "there must be a grand shakeup before long," the fleet steamed north with its command divided. Next stop Callao, port for the Peruvian capital of Lima.

5

▶

Roar of the Big Guns

▶
▶

From Valparaiso to Callao was a six day run of 1,800 miles. As on the fleet's approach to Chile, a native warship, the *Bolognesi,* was sent to greet them 250 miles from their destination.

By now, the officers were dreading their arrival in a South American port. The mobbing crowds, the bands, the frenzied streets—above all, the endless ceremonies—were becoming burdensome and repetitious. Even the battleships looked tired, the poor *Maine* with its coal-grimed decks, the *Alabama* with streaks of yellow from electrolysis on its hull. The dropping of anchors at Callao lacked the precision timing of their previous performances, and drew a reprimand from Evans.

There was no reason to hope for any respite from their host's enthusiasm. Wrote Matthews: "The harbor was crowded with all sorts of little craft laden to the danger point. Every tug, every launch, all the sailboats that could be found, rowing barges, dories, two large oceangoing steamers, came out to say howdy and bearing cheering people by the thousand. Some of the little craft fired national salutes with toy cannon."

There seemed to be confusion on how properly to honor the Americans. One boatload of greeters toured the battleships repeating songs and cheers from Cornell University. But as Matthews wrote, there was no doubt that it all came from the heart.

And there was reason for this exuberance. In South America, Peru was a land without friends. Since gaining independence from Spain in 1821, she had been involved in devastating wars and quarrels with her neighbors. She had lost to Chile the War of the Pacific (1879–84) which the United States had tried to mediate, and was now engaged in a border conflict with Brazil. She needed a friend and ally; she was disposed to look upon the arrival of the fleet as the gesture of a nation come to befriend and "rescue her from ruin."

With this attitude, the government had gone all out in preparation for the visit. Spies had been sent to report on the fleet's reception in Brazil, and Lima was intent on topping it. Bands played a special tune composed for the event; shops posted such signs as "American Spoken Here, Buy a Sewing Machine"; and a troupe of Japanese acrobats performing in the city were thrown into jail out of deference to the Americans.

A local brewer distributed a pamphlet listing "drinks and their prices, Spanish swearwords and how to say them." Lima's principal paper, *El Diario,* hailed in gushing English the United States' "colossal fermentation of greatness," and went on to say: "The United States have many efficacious resources for dissolving or removing indefinitely the threatening and apocalyptic spectre of a universal conflagration such as would take place in the world, given the present aggrupations of factors."

For most of the men the first two days were spent in coaling. Then came Washington's Birthday which conveniently coincided with that of Peruvian President Pardo and which was acknowledged to be "the greatest holiday in history." A reception was held aboard the *Connecticut,* attended by two thousand Peruvian officials. The crush proved so great that three people were pushed overboard, to be rescued by sailors whom Evans subsequently decorated for bravery. President Pardo was invited into Evans' cabin, a courtesy not accorded the presidents of Chile and Brazil, and a flowery telegram was received from Roosevelt which the American president afterwards complained he'd never seen.

Under all this attention, the fleet's officers were growing surly and ill-tempered. "We all dread the hurly-burly," Sperry wrote his wife; while correspondent Robert Dunn complained in *Harper's Weekly*: "O that some scribe would celebrate the urbanity and social endurance of the American naval officer through night after night of dance and dinner, day after day of barbecues and motor rides. He *has* to grace the functions; he is ordered to."

However, two events arranged by the government in honor of the fleet were out of the ordinary, though both were embarrassing fiascos. The first was a bullfight, attended by three thousand officers and men who filled two-thirds of the Plaza de Toros. In deference to the Americans, instructions were given that all goring of the horses was to be avoided. Skilled riders would keep their mounts well away from the bull's horns. But the horses were gored anyway.

The six bulls were named in honor of the fleet and its officers—the connection seemed sometimes obscure, one bull being named "Shufly" for Admiral Sperry—the last on the list being christened "Yankee Doodle" for the men in uniform. In the first engagement, the bull tossed the injured matador out of the ring. In the second two fights, the matador hacked at the bull so unsuccessfully—missing repeated sword thrusts—that the crowd hissed and booed. The next fight was no better, with the matador being gored and left for dead. By this time, many of the Americans were filing out, their sympathies distinctly with the bulls. In his reports to the *Sun,* Franklin Matthews defended the spectacle against charges of cruelty on the grounds that the bulls seemed to enjoy some advantageous odds.

The second event was a ride to the top of towering Mount Oroya on "the highest railroad in the world"—a railroad built by a fugitive embezzler from California. Two trains were engaged, the "official party" going in the first, sailors and nonofficials in the second. At a height of 10,000 feet, the second train was stalled; the official party proceeding further was stricken with vomiting and mountain fever, and laid out prostrate on the floor. The illness proved fatal to one man aboard.

At the top of the mountain, 13,000 feet aloft, word reached the expedition of a landslide that had blocked the tracks below. To remain at that elevation would have caused additional fatalities. The train descended to 10,000 feet, where the unofficial party had appropriated the only inn—ninety men to four available beds. Those aboard the first train slept in their seats, and the next day climbed around the landslide and eventually, sick and exhausted, reached Callao.

It was at Callao that artist-writer Henry Reuterdahl's "heresy" caught up with him. His article in *McClure's,* depicting the battleships' flaws, had by now been well circulated, and he was ordered off the fleet with no provision for returning home. Fortunately a supply ship was on its way to San Diego and he found a berth on her, the captain reporting that he seemed like a man submerged in guilt. His last act was to decorate the decks of the *Connecticut* for a farewell party for Peruvian officials, at which the supplies of candy and hors d'oeuvres ran out, causing Admiral Evans to appeal to Washington for more entertainment funds.

Reuterdahl's charges had already been answered by, among others, naval authority Charles B. Brewer in *Harper's Weekly.* Brewer noted that, as to the submerged armor plate, the ships were necessarily overloaded for the cruise and would be greatly lightened in time of battle. As for the low emplacement of the guns, he did not expect the fleet to fight in a hurricane. As for the exposed magazines, only one accident had occurred so far, that one due to human carelessness. To Reuterdahl's charge that navy bureaucracy had been slow to effect improvements, Brewer admitted, "No truer thing is said by Mr. Reuterdahl than that the system is at fault."

Meanwhile Roosevelt had ordered an investigation of

Reuterdahl's charges by the Senate Committee on Naval Affairs which heard the testimonies of sixty naval experts. As might have been expected, the committee gave the fleet and navy a clean bill of health. One of its more positive suggestions was advanced by Senator Martin who concluded: "It seems to me that if a first-class deserted island can be found in the Pacific, orders should be sent to Admiral Evans to deposit Reuterdahl upon it."

On February 29 the ships were ready to depart. President Pardo positioned his yacht at the mouth of the harbor to review the fleet, and each passing battleship gave him a twenty-one-gun salute. Only one incident marred this farewell pageant. A sailor aboard the *Ohio* had devised a neat plan for deserting. He had hired a small Peruvian boat to follow the *Ohio,* and now jumped overboard and climbed aboard it. As it took off, the next-in-line battleship *Georgia* lowered a launch in pursuit. There followed a helter-skelter chase about the harbor, till the recalcitrant sailor was caught and hoisted aboard his ship—the diplomatic President Pardo pretending to have noticed nothing.

Headed for Magdalena Bay on the western coast of Baja California, the fleet could feel that its obligations to South America had been fulfilled. There were still a few countries clamoring for visits. Ecuador was starboard of their route, and asked for at least a swerve into the Gulf of Guayaquil, similar to that at Valparaiso. The request was twice refused.

Colombia, once New Granada, was an altogether different problem. As the only country in the hemisphere distinctly hostile to the United States, she would have hotly resented a visit from the fleet. Her hostility sprang, if one remembers, from negotiations for the Panama Canal. When the United States purchased rights for the canal's construction from the defunct French company which had started it, Colombia withheld the rights to the strip of land across the Isthmus which it had granted Ferdinand de Lesseps. Roosevelt would not be thwarted. The canal must go through at any cost; the interests of a two-ocean navy made it imperative.

There was only one solution: the secession of the Isthmus from Colombia. It would be hard to deny that this secession had been brought about by United States machinations. Though the Monroe Doctrine outlawed any interference from foreign countries in Latin American affairs, this did not apply to the colossus to the north. Natives on the Isthmus were inspired to revolt, American warships were sent to their support and to seize the Panama Railway bordering the Canal Zone. By November 4, 1903, the rebellion had been successful, and the Republic of Panama declared its independence of Colombia, almost at the same time granting the United States its requested rights for the Panama Canal. No, Colombia would not have welcomed any visit from the Great White Fleet.

On March 12 the battleships dropped anchors in Magdalena Bay, a barren sea embraced by rocky desert, miles from civilization. Here, as in the Straits of Magellan, was another trap in which they might be ambushed, and the officers were frankly worried. In the process of coaling, more dynamite sticks were found, raising the specter of anarchists in the mines of West Virginia planting explosives in those shipments destined for the Battle Fleet.

Even here, a thousand miles from nowhere, rumors reached them of insidious plots against the fleet. Japanese forces lurked in the surrounding hills; Japanese submarines were moving in to block the bay. Watches were doubled aboard the ships, and men became edgy. When one sentry was found missing from his post and later grilled for an explanation, his answer was: "I don't care if the damn ship explodes!"

But depression lifted when the fleet got down to business. For besides being a coaling stop, Magdalena Bay had been selected as the site for target practice. Fifteen miles long by ten miles wide, and amply deep with no impediments, it was perfect for the purpose. Roosevelt had claimed from the start that the voyage to the Pacific was a training cruise, to school fleet personnel in the exigencies of naval warfare. He was particularly concerned with marksmanship and had inaugurated an annual spring competition, in which prizes and cash bonuses were awarded to gunners according to their skills.

Throughout the cruise, target shooting of a sort had been conducted with rifles mounted on the big guns, aimed at miniature targets. But now was to come the real thing, the annual spring competition, and the sailors welcomed it. They were weary of being on display, weary of sprucing up for visitors, even of being pampered by their hosts ashore. All the way from Lima they had been constructing targets, sewing canvas on immense frames, and looking forward to the firing of big guns. This was business; this was navy business.

The range was laid out in the form of a triangle, with

the target at the apex. Each ship would proceed along the base, firing at the target placed 1,000 yards away. Records would be closely kept to rate the ships in competition, bonuses would be paid to winning crews. But not one word of the results would reach the public—this was too much a measure of the fleet's real might, far more significant than its snow-white, glamorous appearance. Rear Admiral Evans warned the correspondents:

> *No statement of scores shall be forwarded, nor whether ships do well or badly.*
>
> *No comments on the workings of the battery or its appurtenances, including the fire control, shall be forwarded.*

Marine captain Henry Dunn learned the meaning of "the dawn comes up like thunder," when at every daybreak the big guns began to fire. Likewise, Chief Turret Captain Roman J. Miller of the *Vermont* was in his element. As he wrote in his diary, later published as a book:

> *All day long and half the night, the big guns boomed on the target ranges, the great hissing shells tore out across the smooth, unruffled waters of the bay, cutting ragged rents in the white canvas targets and throwing tons of water high in the air like so many living geysers. The men worked with almost frenzied activity in the turrets, casemates, and batteries. The ship steamed round the target ranges, the guns blazing forth as they passed the position buoys and came on the range. The din on board was deafening, the effect electrical and thrilling. Guns of all sizes were fired, from the sharp-barking three-pounders to the ponderous, reverberating eight- and twelve-inch turret guns.*

What Captain Miller could not have reported in perspective was the prevalent use of a phrase revived in the 1968 vernacular. As each shell was loaded in the chamber and the breech slammed to, the popular signal for firing was: "Sock it to 'em!"

Victor Chafee, aboard the flagship *Connecticut,* had his own personal impressions of the exercises: "While at torpedo practice in Magdalena Bay they lost two torpedoes and we had to row all the way around the shore to see if we could find them, but no dice. As that part of Baja California is all sand, with the fossils of whales and big fish, it was something to see."

Cornetist-drummer Ed Holland with the U.S.S. *Virginia*'s band also had recollections of the target practice. "For several weeks we practiced gunnery under steam, night and day. Nearly got one of our own men, one night, too! There was a canvas target on a float, way out. Men had been out to repair it, stitched up the holes, pulled it back up the mast and gone back to their ship. But they left a carpenter behind, and didn't even miss him.

"One of the ships sailed past with her 12-inchers ready to blast, but no target. She held fire, and swung back again. Still couldn't see it.

"Smart guy, that carpenter. He had pulled the canvas down. The raft was too low in the water to see. When they went out to investigate, there he was, sitting on the raft, swinging his legs."

For three weeks the fleet's guns blazed, hurling twenty-five tons of metal at the targets; and while actual scores were not revealed, the gunners achieved 100 per cent gains both in accuracy and rapidity of fire over the 1903 results, when the competition first began. Since the tension during these drills was great they were balanced with a sports program of boat races, baseball games, and fishing contests—in what were among the greatest fishing waters of that coastline. Rear Admiral Evans achieved some sports renown with a record catch of sixty yellowtail, a famous game fish of the area.

The twenty days spent at Magdalena Bay was also a period of stock-taking. Except for the remaining run to San Francisco, their coast-to-coast trip was virtually over. The fleet had come through with flying colors. Scarcely a scratch on any of the battleships. No major mechanical failures. No men lost overboard. No stain of shame on any of the personnel. Sickness, of course, there had been—over 150 hospital cases, and 7 dead. But this had been among a complement of 14,000 men. The statistics might have been the same on shore. True, among the black gang in the engine rooms, casualties had been high—where the 150° heat and other pressures had led to over a score of cases of insanity, an occupational hazard.

Among the voyage's casualties was Rear Admiral Evans. He could no longer sustain the myth of being in command, and doubtless had no wish to. His weight had dropped from 178 to 122. For most of the cruise he had been confined to his cabin, the rheumatic gout growing steadily more painful. On March 14 the *Connecticut* took him north for hot bath and mud treatments at the Palo Robles Spa, the ship immediately speeding back to Magdalena Bay. Before leaving, he recommended to the Navy Department that the

Maine and *Alabama,* the proverbial black sheep of the fleet, be replaced by the newly commissioned *Nebraska* and *Wisconsin*—the substitutions to be made when the fleet reached San Francisco.

With Evans's departure, Rear Admiral Thomas became acting commander-in-chief, and transferred his flag to the *Connecticut.* It was plainer than ever that Evans would shortly have to relinquish his position permanently, with one of the two remaining division commanders probably succeeding him. Sperry, who saw himself quite clearly in that role, got out his knife for Thomas; neither he nor Emory would give the admiral the time of day, and often slyly flouted his authority. Thomas, anything but well himself, carried on bravely with indifference to these slights.

On April 11 the battleships steamed out of Magdalena Bay. From then on, according to marine Captain Davis of the *Ohio,* it was "Paint! Paint! Paint! On deck, down below, bridges, storerooms, cabins, hatches—everything in sight and a lot more not in sight, is having a nice new coat of paint . . . and we shall look like a new ship when we get to home waters."

Ahead lay California, symbol of home to the majority of men, harbinger of dread to the officers. After the crushing receptions at Rio and Callao, the Californian cities, primed for welcome, would be murder.

6

Back to "God's Country"

"Lads, there's where America begins. There's the edge of God's country, and just over the other side, where you see them houses, there is where God's people live."

Such was the cry of a homesick sailor aboard the *Louisiana,* on sighting the shores of California. But it was not the sentiment of officers aboard the fleet. Ahead lay Californian ports and cities buzzing like mosquitoes for attention, ready with open arms to welcome them like conquering heroes. It was not only enthusiasm for their achievement. It was the knowledge, coupled with relief, that the great power of the navy was now focused on their shores, and the Yellow Peril of Japan had been forestalled.

The fact remained, however, that the officers of the fleet were especially weary of receptions and effusive welcomes. Had they come direct from Hampton Roads to California their tastes in such matters would have been less jaded by experience. Now, as the *New York Times* observed with sympathy, "When you've been fandangoed under four flags in as many oceans, you've had it."

The anchors dropped first at San Diego, where a boat carrying 33,000 oranges came to welcome them. "The tars greeted the boat with loud cheers and the oranges with eager mouths," the press reported.

Another boat, filled with the town's most beautiful girls, carried flowers to the ships. Doubtless they were greeted even more effusively. Apprehensive of Californian hospitality, Thomas sent a request to the authorities that free drinks to the men be limited, and the word was passed on to the local bars. "Those who came off the ships, however," wrote one news correspondent, "say that the blue jackets have been saving up their thirsts for so long that there is not enough beer in Southern California to slake them."

The principal event at San Diego was a mile-long parade in which 5,000 of the officers and men took part. At its termination at City Hall, Admirals Sperry and Emory were decorated with gold medals, while Admiral Thomas received, on behalf of Evans, a gold key to the city and two swords with gold hilts mounted with red tourmalines. In his speech of acceptance, Thomas paid a gracious tribute to his missing commander. "Whenever the fleet appears without its chief, it is much like presenting the play of 'Hamlet' with the character of Hamlet omitted." After three more days of banquets, balls, and receptions, the fleet weighed anchor for Los Angeles.

To cover the four ports of Los Angeles—San Pedro, Redondo, Long Beach, and Santa Monica—though each demanded the full treatment, Thomas separated the fleet into its four divisions, sending one to each. Long Beach was selected as the site of ceremonies for Los Angeles, where visitors swarmed aboard the ships, many falling overboard in the pressure of the crowd. Overhead, a daredevil balloonist "opened his white parachute, aimed at the after funnel of the *Kearsage,* and almost hit it." Had he succeeded in his aim, this one-man reception committee would have perished for the cause.

The city of Los Angeles, however, was the target of the sailors. They were home now, and restraints were lifted. Girls swarmed the streets in dresses of red, white, and blue, and were liberal with kisses. Clergymen ranted at the "boozy, crushing delirium." Wild West shows and rodeos were staged especially for the fleet. Heavyweight champion Jim Jeffries entertained the men with free beer at his bar, while 3,000 sailors were given auto rides about the city— which included a tour of Hollywood, "a community noted for its vast groves of orange, lemon, fig, and olive trees."

Wrote bandmaster Devine of the *New Jersey*: "Papers stated that the bluejackets owned the city, and we did. The sports opened at Chutes Park, admission gratis. Four days' barbecues and dinners, admission gratis. Best seats at the ringside at the boxing contests, also free. We could spend the remainder of the cruise here (what will old New York and Philly think when they hear of this!). Quite a few overstayed their leave, do you blame them?"

Only one thing marred the celebrations. "The vacant chair in the midst of the Rose Garden in the Alexandria Hotel, where banquets for the officers were given, put a tear in many an eye. But the daily messages from Palo Robles, telling of our Admiral's improvement, were consol ing, and added to the merry-making."

Santa Barbara, next on the schedule of visits, offered a scaled-down version of the Rio de Janeiro riot. A restaurant selling nickel beer upped the price to fifty cents to take advantage of the flood of customers. The sailors responded by tearing the place apart, beam by beam, till taken in charge by the shore patrol. By way of atonement, Admiral Thomas consented to be the leading exhibit in the rose parade, "riding on a flowery float drawn by six white horses."

Santa Cruz and Monterey were each accorded a visit from the battleships, though some trouble was encountered at the latter. Writes Robert Hart: "A gale swept the unprotected anchorage, breaking the *Illinois* off her chain and blowing her half a mile through the formation. Again the fleet was lucky. Emergency anchors caught just as she was about to strike the *Alabama*. So narrow was the miss that the latter's gangway was sheared off and Admiral Sperry's barge crushed between the hulls."

Of all the celebrations on the coast, that at San Francisco was perhaps the most significant and fitting. Even the arrival of contestants in the New York to Paris automobile race took second place to the event. This was the official terminus of the first half of the cruise; and here the "Sweet Sixteen" and their escorts were joined by the eight cruisers of the Pacific Fleet and some forty-odd gunboats and torpedo boats to form a vast parade of warships filing through the Golden Gate—the greatest assembly of naval vessels ever seen, till then, in the United States.

Secretary of the Navy Metcalf had arrived to review the procession from the gunboat *Yorktown,* but the chief figure on hand for the occasion was Rear Admiral Evans. Carried aboard the *Connecticut* at Monterey, he was now in San

Poor health caused Admiral Evans to leave his post as commander-in-chief of the Fleet

Francisco and this was to be his hour of triumph. "I am a new man today," he told reporters. "Didn't I say I'd lead the fleet through the Golden Gate."

But Evans spoke too soon. The bitterest possible moment in an officer's naval career awaited him. His physician ordered him confined to his hotel room. He might ride in parades, but he could not climb the bridge of his beloved flagship. Thomas led the fleet in the review.

It was barely more than a year before that San Francisco had been wracked by an earthquake and fires which had ruined 490 city blocks and left 225,000 persons homeless. Even now marks of the disaster were apparent, but nothing repressed the enthusiasm of its citizens, who had erected a fifty-foot-high electric sign on Telegraph Hill spelling out "Welcome". The million people who lined the streets as six thousand sailors paraded with army troops and the State National Guard clamored for Fighting Bob Evans and threw flowers until he was often chest-deep in roses. "His naval sun went down that day in a veritable blaze of glory."

On May 8 Evans spoke at a banquet in honor of Secretary Metcalf and officers of the fleet. For "the peace of the world" he appealed for "more battleships and fewer statesmen." A day later, he officially relinquished his command and Rear Admiral Thomas moved his flag to the *Connecticut*. Thomas himself, however, was ill and broken by the burdens of the voyage. He held the post of commander-in-chief for only five days, when it passed, by Roosevelt's order, to the covetous Sperry. In less than two months Thomas collapsed and died. Like Evans he had sacrificed his strength and health to the mission of the Great White Fleet.

On the second week in May the fleet moved up the coast to visit Seattle and Tacoma, where California's enthusiastic reception was repeated and where the sailors were presented with live northwestern "Teddy" bears in honor of the president. A month later they were back in San Francisco. No longer burdened with festivities, they got down now to the grimmer business of preparing for the voyage ahead—painting, drydock repairing, taking on coal and supplies for the cruise to the Orient and thence around the hemisphere.

While the plan to send the fleet around the world had been revealed to the officers and men on leaving Hampton Roads, it had, at first, been only a matter of speculation with the public. Roosevelt's orders had surely leaked out in letters written home by sailors, but this was hardly official confirmation. On February 21 the *New York Times* reported, "The eventual movements of our fleet have not yet been determined," but, going on to quote Secretary of State Root, "it is probable that the vessels will return by way of Suez . . . but it would be premature to promise this." In subsequent weeks observant reporters noted heavy shipments of coal to Manila, indicating at least an extension of the cruise, and also the appearance at the Navy Department of an official engaged in supplying ships that passed through the Suez Canal.

Singularly enough another strong hint of the fleet's intentions, or possibly a hazarded guess, came from the Japanese Embassy in Washington where Baron Kogoro Takahira "endorsed the desire expressed by the Japanese press that the fleet under Rear Admiral Evans shall visit Japanese waters on its way to the Atlantic from the Pacific."

Now the round-the-world project was official, though lacking the endorsement of Congress which by rights should have its say in such an undertaking. Roosevelt gave little thought to Congress. If it withheld funds for the remainder of the voyage, he would simply get the ships over there and let Congress figure out a way to get them back.

The extension of the cruise, however, presented another set of problems similar to, but far more complicated, than those encountered on the voyage round South America. Even before the fleet had left the Straits of Magellan, Australia had caught wind of its extended plans and began at once to clamor for the honor of a call. Like Americans on the West Coast she was apprehensive of Japan. A visit from the fleet would be an expression of Australian-American solidarity in the face of a potential enemy.

But Australia was a Crown commonwealth, and Britain was an ally of Japan. Such a visit, reasoned London, would almost certainly antagonize the Japanese, whose citizens had been roughed up in Australia as they had in California. The Australians, however, remained persistent. There was strong feeling in that country that their destiny was linked with the United States, even if this meant secession from the Crown. To quell any thought of the latter, the British government yielded to the pressure and reluctantly sanctioned a visit from the fleet—not only to Australia but to New Zealand as well, which was quick to take advantage of the situation.

How, then, could Great Britain reconcile Japan to these offensive visits? Here skilled diplomacy came into play. It suggested that the Great White Fleet should dispel any thought of partiality by visiting Japan as well—a daring but dramatic gesture. Probably under pressure from its British allies, but perhaps acting on its own appraisal of the situation, the Japanese ambassador in Washington dispatched a note to Roosevelt:

The Imperial Government is firmly convinced of the reassuring effect which the visit of the American fleet to the shores of Japan will produce upon the traditional relations of good understanding and mutual sympathy which so happily exist between the two nations.

This was precisely what Roosevelt wanted, to call on a potential enemy while peace prevailed and demonstrate at close quarters the might of the American navy. There were many in the United States who felt that such a maneuver was rash and might well lead to disaster. Even Admiral Sperry had his doubts and requested, in vain again, that the battleships be painted gray in case of war. In Germany the kaiser was delighted, hoping that the worst might happen, and that war between Japan and the United States would further the German-American alliance.

To Rear Admiral Sperry, new to his command, the situation offered a king-size dilemma. To take his ships into the very waters where the Japanese had lately and overwhelmingly defeated the Imperial Russian Fleet, seemed utter folly. Yet the alternative, he realized, was almost worse. Not to go would suggest that the Great White Fleet was frightened of the Mikado's navy. It would be not just a discourteous and even hostile snub; it would be an admission that the Rising Sun could intimidate America in the Pacific.

If the fleet were to visit Japan, however, how about China, friendly to the United States and bitterly hostile to Japan? She too must be reassured regarding the fleet's intentions. In 1900 the United States had reaffirmed its support of the "Open Door" policy that would "preserve China's territorial and administrative entity" and safeguard "the principle of equal and impartial trade with all parts of the Chinese Empire." Now it was up to the United States to support this policy with evidence of good intentions.

China had already made her move. Hearing that the ships were to visit Japan, the Dowager Empress had promptly invited the fleet to visit China. This left the United States with little choice; the invitation was accepted —thus creating a situation in which both nations, enemies to one another, would be treated equally.

The fleet was ready to put to sea again the first week in July. On the recommendation which Evans had made two months before, two new battleships, the *Nebraska* and the *Wisconsin,* took the places of the decrepit *Alabama* and the coal-devouring *Maine.* To further improve appearances the *Minnesota* switched positions with the *Louisiana,* placing all the better looking ships in Sperry's first division. Otherwise, the composition of the fleet remained the same.

Their itinerary, at this point tentative but as it finally worked out, was:

Hawaii	July 16, 1908
Auckland, New Zealand	Aug. 7
Sydney, Australia	Aug. 20
Melbourne, Australia	Aug. 29
Manila, Philippines	Oct. 1
Yokohama, Japan	Oct. 18
Manila (all but Second Division)	Oct. 31
Amoy, China (Second Division)	Oct. 30
Manila (all Divisions reassemble)	Nov. 7
Colombo, Ceylon	Dec. 14
Suez, Egypt	Jan. 3, 1909
Port Said, Egypt	Jan. 5
Mediterranean ports	Jan. 10–Feb. 1
Gibraltar	Feb. 1
Hampton Roads, U.S.A.	Feb. 22

On July 7 the fleet moved through the Golden Gate and westward out to sea. There was one ship missing from the line, *Nebraska*. As Ensign Eugene Lynch wrote: "We had scarlet fever, mumps, and what have you (diphtheria was also found aboard). We were ordered to Angel Island and were quarantined. We went ashore. First our bags and hammocks were fumigated, then our clothes. We had to go through a needle shower, and then we had supper: hot dogs, potato salad, sauerkraut, corn bread and tea." It was arranged to have the *Nebraska* join the others in Hawaii.

That evening at sea, Sperry opened his sailing orders from the president, revealing his planned itinerary. Simultaneously he received a wireless message:

I send to you and the officers and enlisted men under you, my heartiest good wishes on the eve of your departure. That the American people can trust the skilled efficiency and devotion of its representatives in the fleet, as has been abundantly shown by the trip around South America, will be made manifest on the return trip across the Pacific, Indian, and Atlantic Oceans.

You have in a peculiar sense the honor of the United States in your keeping, and therefore no body of men in the world enjoy at this moment a greater privilege or carry a greater responsibility.

THEODORE ROOSEVELT

7

►

Pacific Island Mission

►
►

There was a sense of destiny aboard the fleet as the ships moved west across the broad Pacific. Except for the conquered hazards of the straits, there had been no high-tension feeling of adventure in their course round South America. It was all one continent attached to the United States, a trip from East Coast home to West Coast home. An expected friendliness and sense of fraternity had met them almost everywhere. There were no unknown or veiled hostilities to be encountered.

But this was different. Only since the midcentury acquisition of California and Oregon, and the later completion of a transcontinental railway, had the Pacific become an "American ocean" and a challenge to the advocates of American expansion. The Spanish-American War of 1898 had suddenly made the United States a Pacific power, with island possessions scattered to the very threshold of Japan. This, and all its implications, took a little getting used to. It changed the mission of the fleet from one of pageantry to serious diplomacy. If that diplomacy should fail, then anything might happen.

With this in mind, Rear Admiral Sperry tightened the

discipline aboard the fleet. For four hours a day he put the ships through intricate maneuvers, forming squares and diamonds, "crossing the T" (in which one line of battleships steamed at right angles across the path of an approaching line, all calling for precision timing), and practicing S formations for entering harbors. These S maneuvers, navy brass believed, not only raised impressive clouds of foam but to those observing, added a sense of three-dimensional depth, accentuating the fleet's size.

On July 16 they sighted the Hawaiian Islands, a significant part of the extended cruise plan. Just ten years previous, in 1898, the islands had fallen conveniently to the United States, following a revolution engineered by American businessmen and planters. The stately Queen Liliuokalani—she who had composed the haunting island song *Aloha Oe*—had been deposed, ending a venerable dynasty, and her possessions had been plundered by unruly mercenaries. At home, in America, there had been considerable opposition to the annexation of the islands, and a feeling of guilt at the mistreatment of the queen. Perhaps a visit from the fleet would help to put things right, or at least confirm the incontestable possession of the islands.

On orders from Secretary Metcalf, the ships in single file swerved past the leper settlement on Molokai "so that the most forlorn people of the world may have an opportunity to see the fleet." At four miles distance the men aboard could see little of the stricken people, but Jesuit brothers at the colony dispatched a wireless of thanks to Sperry for "this brief nod." "Our abode has been called 'Molokai the Blest.' It surely has been blest this day."

The Third Division had not participated in this pageant,

Rear Admiral Emory had turned south with his squad of ships to call at the village of Lahaina on Maui. There were two reasons or excuses for this visit to the tiny "Home of the Hawaiian Kings." Lahaina had requested it, and it was a place where Emory could take on coal. Perhaps the real reason centered on Queen Liliuokalani. Learning of the fleet's approach, still proud and intransigent towards her usurpers, she had retreated to a friend's home in Lahaina. Here she hoped to pass unnoticed. It was Emory's task to appease the queen, or at least make her aware of America's irreversible presence on her islands.

A small detachment of officers from the Third Division, headed by the admiral, called at the queen's abode, and Liliuokalani finally consented to receive them. Her tall and regal presence seemed to make pygmies of the visitors. She held her hand outstretched at shoulder height so that all should reach up to clasp it. She spoke in a soft musical voice of her love for the islands and for the things that had been stolen from her. When Emory turned the conversation to Japan, reminding her that were the islands unprotected the Japanese might well have attacked and overrun them, she said only: "In that case, your people would have been here too, no?"

Dissatisfied that no reconciliation had been made, Emory left to join the balance of the fleet at Honolulu, official site of their reception. As the main fleet had approached Oahu a barrage of daytime fireworks saluted them, "a shower of bombs shooting heavenward, only to burst high in the air displaying beautiful figures and artistic emblems." To the fleet's amazement these pyrotechnics, it appeared, were handled by "enthusiastic Japanese." Could this be possible, such demonstrative attention from the secret enemy? It was only later learned that the date, July 16, was Japanese Day on the island, and the fireworks had only chance association with the fleet's arrival.

Actually their reception, at least on the part of the natives, was restrained. After their initial banzai blast, the 25,000 Japanese of Oahu remained in seclusion, as did much of the Polynesian population. Only the Anglo-Saxon residents went all out in their welcome—with the customary bands and decorations and the promises of native female charm. One E. S. Goodhue, poet laureate of the islands, composed a poem for the event, of which the last two stanzas ran:

> *Voices of maidens here are low,*
> *Musical, soft and sweet,*
> *Charming the ear with their cadences—*
> *Boys of the noble fleet.*

> *Nowhere are smiles more genuine,*
> *Nowhere are hearts more glad;*
> *Welcome from every isle of us.*
> *Welcome, each sailor lad.*

For the planned parade of 2,500 bluejackets through the streets of Honolulu, the wives of local businessmen suggested that the sailors carry leis around their necks, and organized a troupe of hula maidens to distribute them. To this, the editor of the Honolulu *Advertiser* hastily added his suggestion:

It has always seemed to us that instead of carrying a rude, dangerous gun on a holiday march the sailor would look more becoming if he should carry a calla lily or a small geranium in a pot. And it would be too sweet for anything if the members of the bands would carry a singing bird in a cage. Then all along the way little girls with spray-bottles could perfume our proud boys in blue and give each officer a ribboned syphon full of some of our delicious island scents so he could renew the perfume at intervals during the march. And where the dear fellows stop to rest each one should have ice cream with nuts on top.

The sailors marched without the leis, and with bayonets gleaming from their rifles. But when the parade was over and the sailors halted at the dock, the still undaunted band of hula girls, equipped with leis, "charged on them, hooped their necks with the wreaths, and put the lads in the finest possible humor."

Those with shore leave visited Diamond Head and the gun emplacements being built around Pearl Harbor. In 1887 King Kalakaua, the deposed queen's predecessor, had granted the United States exclusive use of the harbor for coaling and naval repairs, in return for certain sugar concessions. Now the navy was spending $3,000,000 with more to come on fortifying its shores and widening and deepening the harbor. It was an' ideal base, the men agreed, for offensive action in the North Pacific, and sufficiently remote to be secure from attack. With the American flag high over the Pacific, and American ships patrolling the ocean, the Japanese would never reach these islands.

Before leaving Honolulu the fleet was rejoined by the

fumigated *Nebraska*. There would still be a hole in the ranks, however, for the *Minnesota* remained behind to receive mail due from San Francisco. The receipt of mail was vital to the fleet's morale, and at no time was it overlooked for the sake of naval expediency. Right now morale had suffered somewhat under Sperry's stringent discipline. Dubbed "Speedy Sperry" for his having raised the cruising speed from ten to eleven knots and greater, he had added a new maneuver to their daily drills: to the figure S, he added a new twist, the loop. Twin lines of battleships would curve, respectively, to left and right, make a complete circle, and resume their precise position in the line.

It was a tricky maneuver, almost causing the first ship fatality of the cruise. Completing its loop and returning to the line, the *New Jersey* miscalculated and crashed into *Nebraska*'s beam, its long ram slicing through the latter's bow. Sperry called a halt while the *Nebraska* underwent repairs, and news of the misadventure was suppressed. There had been no crew fatalities or injuries, and the collision passed unnoticed by the world.

The run from Honolulu to New Zealand, seventeen full sailing days, was the longest of the fleet's entire voyage. The danger of the crews becoming restless through this long restraint was met by providing extra entertainment for off-duty hours. Boxing and fencing matches were arranged, chess and checker boards were brought out, minstrel shows were organized and dramatic groups performed. Each ship had its supply of costumes, with a collapsible stage to be erected in the bow. Aboard the *Vermont* a typical venture in theatrics was reviewed:

PROGRAMME

1. The Brass Band of the *Vermont* rendered a fine Overture which was called for again and again.

2. Stereopticon Views, entitled "A Trip to Niagara Falls," a very realistic production.

3. Illustrated Song entitled "And a little child shall lead them" sung by Wallace, seaman U.S.S. *Vermont*. Wallace, who has an exceedingly fine and cultivated voice, was obliged to respond to repeated encores.

4. Fencing Contest, J. J. Keegan and F. M. Connor, was considered a good example of "Jack's" ability with the foils.

5. Selection by the Brass Band of the *Vermont*.

6. Illustrated Song by J. B. Broderick, U.S.M.C., entitled "When the violets whisper, sweet Marie." This was undoubtedly the hit of the evening, appealing very strongly to all, as on that day we had received in mid-ocean our mail from home.

7. Boxing Bout, F. W. O. Mahoney and W. C. Murphy. This number was very exciting and interesting.

8. Stereopticon View, "Piker's Dream," was the last number of the regular programme, and the band concert which followed concluded a most enjoyable entertainment.

On the first of August they came abreast of the Samoan group of islands, now peacefully divided between Germany and the United States after being a near source of war between them. The German harbor of Apia would shortly shelter the Pacific Fleet and the torpedo boat flotilla, hither bound from San Francisco and under instructions to stand by for trouble when the Battle Fleet entered Japanese waters. At this point only a single United States gunboat, the *Annapolis,* rested in the harbor. The fleet granted it the courtesy of a salute, and passed on. In similar manner it bypassed the Fiji Islands whose inhabitants had gone to great lengths to prepare a welcome for the sailors in the false hope that the fleet would stop.

There followed three days of heavy weather—the worst seas that the battleships had yet encountered since leaving Hampton Roads. The Big Sixteen ploughed its way through twenty-foot-high waves that crashed against their forecastles. It reached its peak the evening of August 7 when Captain R. J. Miller observed: "The night was dark; heavy, black, rolling clouds muffled the sky in the early evening, and later not a spark of light was visible in any direction other than the ships' running lights, and they but dimly. We listened intently to the shrieking of the wind as it tore through the rigging, and to the long hiss of the waves rushing past us with lightning speed. Sometimes an avalanche of foam buried us for a moment, even the powerful *Vermont* trembling under the blow."

The ships had carried extra coal on deck to provide for the long run to New Zealand. Now they were streaked with black from the water that drenched the sacks. All this would have to be scrubbed away, the hulls repainted and brass polished bright, for they were approaching British waters. Still smarting from the English snub at Trinidad, acutely conscious of the British claim to superiority at sea, the officers were determined to put on a flawless show at Auckland, principal city of New Zealand. An order went out prohibiting the use of cigarettes and chewing gum ashore (Sperry had already closed the canteens selling cigarettes and candy when he'd discovered that sailors in charge had been pocketing the profits).

At Auckland, Sperry met his first important test in the face of British appraisement. Robert Hart wrote: "The fleet formed single-file and increased speed to thirteen knots to 'get good foam at the bows.' Sperry signalled for the new S formation, the snaking movement designed to enhance perspective. Three-dimensional effects were superb, and the 'Entry to Auckland' was to become a best-selling stereopticon slide. The line broke and formed divisional squares 'with all the precision of a Guards regiment.' Sixteen engines backed and stopped, sixteen anchors plunged, sixteen jacks caught the wind, and sixty-four guns opened the saluting. Emory described Sperry's satisfaction. He had 'never seen anything better done or anything that gave him more pleasure, particularly as it was done in the presence of the English fleet.' "

The show was wasted on the English naval units which they found at Auckland. Only three outmoded British cruisers lay at anchor in the harbor, their polite salute drowned out by the din of welcome from surrounding craft. Seaman Devine on the *New Jersey* waxed indignant that this "fleet's" commanding officer, Vice-Admiral Coore, ranked higher than Rear Admiral Sperry. "Once more," he wrote, "we saw a lesser fleet commanded by an officer of greater rank than the Commander-in-Chief of this, the greatest fleet ever seen in these waters. . . . Some may live to see the fleet commanded by an officer of commensurate rank, with the dignity of the United States."

To describe the fleet's welcome to New Zealand, Franklin Matthews coined a word, "fleetitis." It referred to the mad enthusiasm which infected Auckland's population on its first view of the fleet. The city's blue laws were suspended for the week; Queen Street, the leading thoroughfare, was "a bower from end to end" with flowers, flags, and arches; Rear Admiral Sperry was so much in demand that he had to make eight speeches in a single day. A champagne reception aboard the *Louisiana,* attended by three thousand guests, brought an extraordinary rebuke from the commanding officer. It had cost only $438. Why hadn't more been spent—to impress these British subjects properly?

At Auckland the officers and sailors of the fleet were confronted with a new interpretation of their mission. They had come to the South Pacific, they were told, as the predestined saviors of Australasia. England, the mother country, was too remote to champion the cause of Australasia for the white man and the white man only. Between the islands of New Zealand and Australia, and the emigrating hordes of Japanese, the Battle Fleet of the United States presented a potential barrier.

This Down Under attitude was recognized in England, where the *London Daily Chronicle* reported: "The popular rejoicings in New Zealand are primarily and sincerely a demonstration of friendship for the United States. They are also the background for a demonstration against Oriental immigration in the white man's lands."

Included in the week of celebration was a visit to inland Rotorua, home of the fierce Maori tribesmen, "the only savage people in the world never conquered by the white man." Sperry was greeted by a Maori chieftan who embarrassed him by shouting "Bully!" through a buck-toothed mask of Teddy Roosevelt. But with grim good nature he allowed himself to be decked in Maori battle dress, with a kiwi feather mat about his shoulders, wide leather war belts round his waist, and a Maori spear in each hand.

Thus attired, he was addressed by the Maori chieftain who assured him, with what could have been *double entendre*: "We especially welcome you because the Maoris are a seafaring people and in the olden days, when your ancestors were hugging the coasts, they sailed in canoes all over the Pacific Ocean."

New Zealand, the sailors found, had everything. Though this was winter in the southern hemisphere, the climate was soft and mild, and palm trees lined the streets of Auckland. Inland was every type of scenery that the United States could boast, and some it could not: towering alps and plunging glaciers, Norwegian fjords, lush jungle forests, rivers and trout-filled streams and waterfalls. And in between, a replica of the green New England countryside to make a Yankee seaman homesick. Its charm led to a near-disaster.

On the eve of their departure, a band of local singers gathered at the wharf to serenade the fleet with "Auld Lang Syne." They were treated to a bit of unprepared excitement. A number of recalcitrant sailors had decided to adopt New Zealand as their home, and were being forcibly propelled aboard their ships by members of the shore patrol. Well-meaning New Zealanders swarmed to the sailors' rescue, battling their captors. Only by threatening the crowd with their revolvers could the shore patrol succeed in getting the deserters to their ships—a melee that was gleefully reported by the London press.

There was more orderly excitement when they sailed the following morning, August 15, for Sydney. The *New York Times* reported: "As the ships hoisted anchor, pandemonium reigned. The shore batteries belched forth parting salutes, which were answered by the American ships, and the whistles and sirens on the excursion flotilla resounded across the harbor. The sight when the ships left their anchorage was a magnificent one, the flagship *Connecticut* turning and steaming between the lines of battleships, which turned in order and followed it to sea."

8

Hospitality
Down Under

"And now begins the important part of the war or peace drama—the demonstration against Japan."

So commented the German *Karlsbad Badeblatt* in anticipation of the Great White Fleet's arrival in Australia. It was a presumptuous statement, reflecting the kaiser's hope for a Japanese-American conflict touched off by the cruise. Far removed from American purpose—this was no "demonstration against Japan"—it nevertheless conformed to the Australian attitude. Like California, Australians lived in exaggerated terror of the Yellow Peril.

Australia's fears were not entirely unwarranted. This largest island on the globe lay due south of the Japanese and Chinese coastlines, behind which abounded two-thirds of the world's population. Her vast and empty areas were tempting targets for those overcrowded countries. Cheap Japanese and coolie labor poured into the Commonwealth; and because of England's friendship for Japan, Australia could not do much about it beyond harboring resentment and letting off steam in anti-Japanese demonstrations.

Now she hailed the arrival of the fleet as a warning to

Japan that further invasion of her shores would not be welcome. Here was proof that she and the United States stood shoulder to shoulder in protecting Australia's integrity as "a white man's country." The last two lines of a currently popular poem reflected these passionate sentiments:

> For the sake of our race of the future
> Hail! Men of America, Hail!

While all this was embarrassing to Washington officials and to officers aboard the fleet, it accounted in large degree for the "fleet frenzy" that possessed the citizens of Sydney. "All their reserve energy and heartiness apparently had been bottled up for weeks and months, and it was let loose with the force of a volcanic explosion when the fleet arrived."

In fact, Sydney couldn't wait for the arrival of the fleet. Even before daybreak, thirty miles at sea, Sperry's searchlights singled out a steamer coming towards them in the dark, laden with well-wishers. Then another. And another. By daybreak, a dozen ocean-going steamers, crowded with "madly waving people," swarmed around the battleships. From nearer shore came the proverbial excursion boats and pleasure craft with the customary flags and bunting. The only fresh touch to this now familiar scene was a school of whales which lined up at the entrance to the harbor and obligingly spouted "streams of water high into the air" to contribute to the general jubilation.

The waterborne crowds were so great that Sperry was advised by the authorities to stay at sea until the harbor could be cleared—a situation reminiscent of the crowds at the *America*'s Cup races, then held off Sandy Hook. The battleships loafed along outside the harbor, giving the men a view of "thousands upon thousands" of civilians perched along the bluffs. "The high cliffs and stony declivities were simply a mass of human beings; they were like the pictures of so many thousands of wild birds on rocks and headlands, pictures that have been brought to us at times from explorers in the high seas."

When the first landing parties touched on shore they found the city decorated even more elaborately than at Auckland. The *Vermont*'s Chief Turret Captain Roman Miller noted "a perfect wealth of flags, drapings and hangings, banners, standards, and signals, enswathing whole streets, half covering great blocks. From end to end of the principal streets we walked beneath a trellis of festoons, while canopies of broad colored silks appeared everywhere." At the head of King Street a five-story replica of the Statue of Liberty towered above the visitors.

"We came, we saw, we conquered!" wrote bandmaster Devine of the *New Jersey*. "We must award the palm to the Australians, as having tendered us the grandest reception we have yet seen. Los Angeles has, and always will have, a proud place in the hearts of the men of the Atlantic Fleet, but Sydney has, by its supreme efforts, succeeded in wrestling the honors of entertaining away from her."

Bandmaster Devine must have had a strong stomach for entertainment. For by now the constantly repeated jovialities, so much the same in every port, had assumed a devastating sameness. The bluejackets paraded; innumerable

Crowds gathered to watch as the Fleet entered Sydney Harbor

bands did their perspiring best with "The Star-Spangled Banner"; Sperry attended countless banquets and topped his record with thirteen speeches in a single day. A special song composed in honor of the fleet and called "Big Brother" was dinned interminably into everybody's ears.

News of the brawl on the docks at Auckland had preceded their arrival, along with rumors that American seamen got out of hand when granted liberty. Quietly the city took police precautions, and the authorities requested that the bluejackets parade without arms. Sperry considered the request ridiculous; his men would look like "clowns" without their rifles, and he ordered that they carry them.

Actually, the sailors behaved well at Sydney (though merchants complained that some passed Confederate money). Many Yankees found that the city, with its narrow streets and central Common, reminded them of Boston—"Downeasters felt right at home," wrote Matthews— and one sailor was heard to remark "Gee, this looks so much like home that I think I'll go out to some place or other and ask for a plate of Boston baked beans." The Sydney *Mail* kindly called the visit, "the greatest national picnic that Australia has ever known." When the time came for parting on August 27, the crowds which assembled to see them off matched those which had greeted them the week before. One steamer, loaded with well-wishing Sydneyites, followed them for a day and a night on their southward run to Melbourne.

Perhaps because of jealously between Australia's leading cities and the fact that both regarded the fleet's appearance as a warning to Japan, the reception at Melbourne during what was known as "American Week" topped, in exuberance and frenzy, any that had gone before. Matthews compared it to "a colossal merry-go-round . . . with 14,000 American sailors near the rim." Of the innumerable marching bands that came to greet them, he had only one complaint: "Some one ought to teach them to play 'The Star-Spangled Banner.' . . . It was a jig from the start with a rush to get through as quickly as possible."

Melbourne's "implacable hospitality" jeopardized many a naval career. Officers ordered to appear at certain ceremonies found the crowds so great that they could not reach their destinations. The customary parade of bluejackets was sadly blurred by too much beer. Sailors strayed from the ranks to weave in happy oblivion down the streets, while the navy's bands found it hard to keep in step and keep on key. Sperry was furious, and when the reports of this boozy cavalcade reached Roosevelt, one man was discharged and several others were court-martialed.

"Fleetitis" was the obvious explanation for the lapse from order which infected the entire population. Writes Robert Hart in his excellent story of *The Great White Fleet*: "Hospitals were full of people who had been trampled in the streets or had fallen off buildings while watching parades. A grandstand collapsed and a bridge broke down under the weight of the crowds. Two sailors were killed by rampaging trolleys whose motormen seemed infected by the general madness. The victims could not be buried because Melbourne had decreed that there should be no funerals to mar the happiness of the visit."

There was, as already noted, a strong undercurrent to this unrestrained enthusiasm, as there had been at Sydney and at Auckland. "Everywhere you went the Great Dread was uppermost." That Great Dread was focused on the giant powers of the Orient, China and Japan. Great Britain had withdrawn her main fleet from the Pacific, leaving only a handful of cruisers to protect the Commonwealth. The current demonstrations toward Americans were partly aimed, in Melbourne as at Sydney, at impressing the mother country that all of Australasia lived in terror of the Yellow Peril. They looked with distress at England's alliance with Japan. They needed a navy to protect them— if not the British navy, then that of the United States.

Among certain elements these sentiments reached extremes, expressing the thought: Take heed, England! If you fail to recognize our fears, our aspirations for a navy to patrol our shores, we may well turn to the United States, closer to us in both geography and feeling. Some even spoke of secession from the Empire and alliance with America. In subtle ways this thinking was expressed in the words of the song "Big Brother"—played unceasingly in Melbourne as at Sydney—the chorus of which went:

> *We've got a big brother in America,*
> *Uncle Sam! Uncle Sam!*
> *The same old blood, the same old speech,*
> *The same old songs are good for each;*
> *We'll all stand together, boys,*
> *If the foe wants a flutter or a fuss;*
> *And we're hanging out the sign,*
> *From the Leeuwin to the Line:*
> *This bit o' the world belongs to us!*

That Great Britain heeded this outcry was suggested by its view of the Pacific voyage as Roosevelt's "Hurrah Party" which "conforms ill with the present engagements of the Empire." Perhaps because of this only two of the six expected British colliers kept their appointments in Melbourne when it came time to coal the battleships. They simply failed to appear. It may have been a sly suggestion that the fleet was powerless without Great Britain's condescension. The situation was somewhat aggravated when the Melbourne dockworkers went on strike, complaining that American sailors loaded their own vessels. Embarrassed and angry, Sperry had to purchase 16,000 tons of inferior Australian coal to get the ships around to the coaling station of Albany in the southwest corner of the country.

It was a lesson they might have learned in 1905 from the voyage of the Russian Admiral Rozhestvenski's Baltic Fleet, which had sailed halfway around the world to be defeated at Tsushima by the Japanese. Much of its difficulty and delay enroute had been in coaling. Now American officers realized "the necessity of a navy owning its own colliers, as merchant colliers are usually under foreign flags, undependable in peace and much more so in war." Not only that, but in the future the American Navy would have its own coaling stations around the world if it were to operate effectively.

When Matthews compared the week-long celebration at Melbourne to a merry-go-round, with the sailors at the rim, he added: "Wouldn't a lot of those sailors be flung off that great turntable? Well, a lot of them were thrown off." Whether or not he was referring to defections from the fleet the fact remained that desertions in Melbourne reached, for the first time, serious proportions. Over three hundred seamen left their ships, many cajoled by girl friends who concealed them in their homes. Some were rounded up, of course. Of more than two hundred others— many of whom settled down and married under Australia's easy citizenship laws—it was philosophically concluded that they and their expected offspring would help to strengthen the existing ties between Australia and America. As if in support of this contention, a Melbourne admirer of President Roosevelt published this limerick in a local paper:

> *Mr. Teddy, rough and ready,*
> *To the crowd doth cry:*
> *"See the rabbit!*
> *Get the habbit:*
> *Go and multiply!"*

Meanwhile the fleet had lost the equivalent manpower of a Fourth Division battleship—as much as they'd expect to lose in an actual engagement.

Before leaving Melbourne, souvenir medals were presented to every man in the armada, most of whom had lost their cap ribbons, given or snatched by the crowds as souvenirs. They acquired also a menagerie: Australian "Teddy" bears presented to the Yankee visitors in honor of their president. In fact, the loss of personnel was offset by the growing ranks of mascots acquired from port to port: dogs, monkeys, parrots, wallabies, kangaroos, one laughing jackass, and now koala bears. As they sailed from Melbourne to the coaling port of Albany, over the mountainous swells of the South Pacific, seasickness—long since overcome by the enlisted personnel—became an embarrassing plague among the animals.

The "world's greatest roller coaster" was the name the fleet gave to the undulating sea off south Australia, where the world's tides followed the moon around the globe uninterrupted by the continents. As the iron giants rose and fell from peak to trough, the bridge officers struggled to keep their ships in line. On every rise it looked as if the following ship would crash into the one before it. They reached Albany on September 11, and for once no formal welcome awaited them. They had come here of necessity to coal, and their only social obligation was to listen to the song "Big Brother" played on the tinny piano in the town hall. Upon the appearance of a news report that two tons of sausages were being shipped to Albany for their arrival, a local poet produced the lines:

> *Many a Yankee sailorman will glue his Yankee gums*
> *To that which never uttered more than "neigh,"*
> *And the officers will help the sailors bulge their rummy-tums,*
> *With "two tons of sausages a day!"*

When Sperry led the fleet from Albany due north towards Manila, 3,300 miles away, he knew he was facing the crucial test of his career. It had long since been agreed that they would call at Tokyo. But now that that time approached, the world's excitement, and the tension, mounted. Observed the London *Daily Mail,* "The United States . . .

is venturing her head into the jaws of the Japanese lion."
The Paris *Patrie* asked in a headline, "Where Is the Japanese Fleet?" and reported it cruising off Hawaii. Japan alone adopted a posture of shaky reassurance. Japanese Ambassador Kogoro Takahira continued to tell the United States that "war between America and Japan would be a crime against humanity and civilization."

The fleet had been extraordinarily favored by the weather in ten months at sea. Except for being mildly shaken up before and after touching at New Zealand, they had encountered no severe storms in their 20,000 miles of cruising. Now as they steamed north the Pacific continued to live up to its name with constant cloudless skies and quiet seas, and "life on the rolling deep as joyous and entrancing as was ever found." The sailors changed from navy blue to white, and gathered at the rails to view the passing islands of Malaysia—Borneo, Sumatra, Java. Off the coast of Mindanao they were intercepted by two war canoes containing Moro warriors who endeavored to communicate, by a frantic beating of their tom-toms, their good intentions toward the battle fleet.

While the worries inherent in their steady progress far from home and nearing hostile waters still remained, their visit to the Philippines, where the fleet arrived on October 2, had immediate significance. Since acquiring the islands from Spain for $20,000,000 following the war of 1898, the "Philippine Problem" had become a growing headache. What to do with them was the essence of that problem. Let them have their independence and they might easily be swallowed by Germany, Great Britain, or Japan—most likely the latter, since their fortified island of Formosa was only 350 miles away. Besides, had argued President McKinley, the Filipinos were not ready for independence. There was nothing for conscientious Americans to do but rule them with a strong hand, following the widely touted words of Rudyard Kipling:

> *Take up the White Man's burden,*
> *Send forth the best ye breed* . . . .

It was a severe shock to America's self-righteous pride when the Filipinos seemed not to respect the White Man's burden or the rights of "the best ye breed" to govern them. It had taken a two-year war involving 120,000 troops and costing as many lives as the war with Spain to subdue the Filipinos temporarily. They were still in smoldering rebellion in the hills around Manila. Not only that, but back in the United States some second thoughts about the islands were in circulation. Were they really worth the cost and trouble? And among reformers, wasn't our presence there a form of imperialism at its worst?

This left the 5,000 Americans now in Manila, among the city's 25,000 population, with a sense of precarious removal from the mother country. They, the ruling class, were in a pitiful minority, not looked upon with kindness by their "little brown brothers." A visit from the fleet was a desperately desired reassurance that the United States had not deserted them. It would give the recalcitrant Filipinos some idea of the mighty, irreversible force that bolstered the White Man's burden.

But there was to be no visit, as Sperry had directed when he learned at sea of a cholera epidemic that had gripped the islands. There had been some 12,500 deaths out of 21,450 cases in the previous two months. Sperry was taking no chances of exposing his fleet population to this hazard.

In vain the local reception committee argued that the scourge was all but ended, new cases had diminished to but five or ten a day. They pointed to $170,000 spent to deck the city with flags and drapes and build ceremonial arches for the coveted parade of sailors. Tons of perishable food had been imported to feed the anticipated crowds. Sperry remained adamant. A few officers with missions were allowed ashore, instructed to return by 10 P.M. No food or drink or other supplies would be purchased at Manila.

The reaction of the town was understandably resentful. A few excursion vessels cruised around the ships and cheered the sailors at the railings. But other spectators openly hurled insults from the shore, in return for what they considered an insult from the fleet. The American community was, of course, particularly let down. They had lost face to the Filipinos. The impression they had hoped the fleet would make was lost.

The only bright spot to fleet personnel was the receipt of mail from home—an ever-important event, for hundreds of knitted scarves and home-baked pies pursued the men around the world, along with stacks of scented letters from the girls they'd left behind. Cora Randall of Whitman, Massachusetts, reversed the sailor's tradition of a girl in every port and had a man on almost every ship with whom she corresponded sentimentally ("I was much younger then," she reminisced in 1953). And back in reply came snapshots and souvenirs that ranged from medals to vanilla beans. Cora counted among her collection a prayer mat and slippers, a piece of wood from Nelson's sunken ship, some mounted insects, pressed tropical flowers, and Australian seashells. "I also have five hummingbirds and a neckerchief from Rio."

On October 10 they said good-bye to the harbor where, ten years before, Admiral Dewey's victory had brought to ruin the mighty Spanish empire in the New World. Ahead now, as they plunged into the China Sea, lay the critical mission of the voyage. Naval Intelligence had alerted Sperry that Japan was making careful preparations for the visitors. School children were being given American flags and taught to say "I love you" and "E Pluribus Unum." Welcoming arches were going up in Tokyo. But on top of that, with ominous implications, the Imperial Navy—battleships, cruisers, destroyers, torpedo boats, and submarines —had been ordered on maneuvers! In fact it was right now heading south toward the Philippines, one hundred and sixty warships primed for battle.

Sperry at this point could have given many thanks for the American cruisers and torpedo boats supposedly waiting at Samoa. Remarkably, for reasons he would only later learn, these units had been recalled to the West Coast. The fleet was naked of all defenses.

9

Fateful Encounter

What can one expect when two great battle fleets, armed to the teeth and conditioned to regard each other as inevitable enemies, meet head on in the high seas?

What the Great White Fleet actually encountered was what it least expected—the worst typhoon to hit the China Seas in forty years. It had been brewing since they left Manila. On Saturday, October 11 the officer on the bridge looked at the barometer. Falling. Seas high and skies obscured by scudding clouds. Sunday, still falling. Winds of gale proportions. Monday, still falling.

On that day the full fury of the storm engulfed them. Winds reached a hundred miles an hour. Waves sixty feet high lashed at the windows of the bridge with snarling spray, churned round the turrets, flooded the chart rooms fifty feet above the decks. The sea became a dark green, raging no man's land of towering mountains and pitted valleys; it was impossible to see more than the pitching topmasts of the other vessels. "The battleships were tossed around like eggshells," wrote a sailor on the *Kansas*.

As the *Connecticut* slid down the hissing flank of one great wave, deep into the trough, it plunged into the wall of the succeeding wave. Tons of water crashed on deck, shaking the ship from stem to stern and sweeping before it anything not made fast. Watching his fleet fall apart, Sperry ordered all the vessels to heave to, maintaining an engine speed of five knots to combat the wind. For some the order came too late. The *Kearsage* had lost her topmast and therewith her wireless communication and was carried far west to the Loo Choo Islands. The *Illinois* and *Wisconsin* both lost lifeboats and were also carried off. By noon the entire Fourth Division had dropped out of sight.

There was no letup in the debacle. A signal flashed from the *Georgia* told that a gunners mate had been washed overboard and before a lifeboat could be lowered had disappeared. Minutes later the signal for "man overboard" flashed also from the *Minnesota*. Seaman T. H. Gladden, an expert swimmer, struggled to reach the lifelines thrown him from the *Minnesota*'s deck. Still struggling, he was swept back towards the following *Vermont*.

The *Vermont* let Gladden pass its bow, then turned abeam of the wind to give him a protective lee. A boatswain threw him a line, and he was hauled to safety, appearing "as cool and unruffled as if emerging from a pleasant swim." Asked how he had felt out there alone, he answered: "Well, I felt a long way from home." Later in the day another sailor was swept from the foredeck of the *Illinois* and was narrowly hauled from drowning much as Gladden had been rescued.

But gunners mate William Fuller was less lucky. Caught with a companion by a giant wave that swept the *Rhode Island*'s foredeck, where both were trying to make fast the gun racks, they were thrown into the sea. A shipmate Clifford Bemus witnessed the incident and wrote: "Fuller and a seaman by the name of, I think, Bjorenson, were on the main deck trying to secure a gun rack, when the ship lay over on her side and the sea came up so fast they couldn't get away.

"They both were thrown through the netting that is put up in a storm, but Bjorenson managed to reach out and catch hold of it and hold on. When the ship cleared herself of water by rolling on the opposite side, and before the sea came up again, a couple of seamen got a rope around him and pulled him in. But Fuller had gone through the netting and was in the water. Captain Murdock appeared in time to stop the lifeboat crew from dropping into the sea, saying, 'I would rather lose one man than six or eight.' Then Fuller came up 50 or 75 feet from the ship and raised his hand and I thought he hollered, 'So long, fellas.' "

It was impossible to catch a moment's sleep throughout the tempest. Ventilators had been shut tight against the flooding of the decks. The cabins below were suffocating. Wind roared and whistled in the rigging. The crash of falling objects and the pounding of the ship itself kept up a constant and ear-splitting clamor. Wrote seaman Howard Voit aboard the *Kansas*: "I was trying to sleep in my hammock, when a monstrous wave caught our ship and she seemed to stand on end. I thought for a few seconds that the old girl was doomed. I thought if another wave hit her just right, she would roll over. But she fooled us."

There was hardly a ship undamaged by the storm. Lifeboats were smashed or snatched into the sea. Railings were warped and twisted from the decks; windows and ports were shattered. Wireless aerials were destroyed and communications were thrown into confusion. To Sperry, watching sleepless on the bridge of the *Connecticut,* his ships seemed constantly to vanish behind the shifting walls of water.

And what of the admiral's yacht *Yankton,* still valiantly in attendance? Wrote the *Virginia's* Eddie Holland: "She simply disappeared. We figured she was a goner. But at the end of a week, when the storm tapered off, a message came in on the wireless from Cavite in the Philippines. Everybody was safe but the vessel was a wreck. She'd lost both her masts, all the rigging, and was pretty well beaten up topside."

By Tuesday the storm had spent its fury, and the sea subsided to a sheet of sunlit glass. The ships resumed their orderly positions. The crews set about repairing damaged railings, twisted ladders, and the next three days were spent in painting woodwork, polishing brass, and generally sprucing up the ships for their appearance in Yokohama. As they approached Tokyo Bay, through heavy mist, there was no need for anyone to be reminded that somewhere in these waters was the fleet that had destroyed the entire Russian Baltic Fleet just four years before.

Now it was the Americans' turn to ask: Where is the Japanese fleet? As it turned out, they too had been badly battered by the storm and were reassembling slowly in the fleet's wake, later to take up positions at the entrance to Tokyo Bay. Not knowing of this disposition, the Americans were apprehensive, still more apprehensive when three ghostlike warships loomed before them in the mist. The vanguard of an enemy armada? Sperry ordered his crew to battle stations, when he learned that they were Japanese cruisers come to escort the Fleet into the harbor.

The simple act of entering Tokyo Bay had been preceded by a six-months flurry of preparations in the way of diplomatic talks designed to smooth the points of friction between Japan and the United States. In February the two countries had arrived at a "gentlemen's agreement" which limited Japanese emigration to America. A month later work was begun on the Root-Takahiri Treaty to respect each other's territorial rights, meaning for Japan its rights of aggrandizement in Manchuria, and for America, a free hand in the Philippines.

Ostensibly the United States seemed to hold the upper hand in these negotiations. But on many positions she had yielded to unspoken ultimatums from Japan. She had wanted to send a token fleet to Tokyo; Japan had insisted on the whole fleet or none at all. She had wanted to send the whole fleet to her friend and ally, China. Japan had protested that this would make China equal in importance to Japan; only a portion of the fleet should make the visit. The United States agreed. Finally, Japan regarded the presence of the Pacific Fleet at Samoa, while the Atlantic Fleet was at Tokyo, a gesture of hostility. Metcalf called the Samoan ships home. For once Roosevelt's habitual firmness seemed to have softened in the face of an emergency.

On October 15 the *New York Times* reported: "All Japan is astir in anticipation of the arrival of the Americans. Yokohama, and Tokyo in particular, are given over to enthusiastic preparation. The decorations in these cities are so extensive as to be remarkable not only in Japan, but in any country of the world. All the Japanese newspapers are printing editions in English, with long editorials assuring the American officers and sailors of a hearty welcome by the natives."

Coupled with this encouraging news came the report that Japan had cancelled plans for its 1912 World Exposition. The vacated fair grounds would be used for drilling troops. This might or might not have significance, but Roosevelt had regarded the forthcoming exposition as a warranty of peace. Now that warranty had been revoked.

The fleet's entrance into Tokyo's port of Yokohama was correct and disciplined. "Storm-battered but magnificent," the battleships made "a display unprecedented in the history of Yokohama." They dropped anchor, as directed, beside sixteen corresponding warships of the emperor's navy which had been appointed to serve as "mates" to the Americans. The customary salutes were given. The men dressed arms at the rails and stared at one another. Seaman Ambrose Jones of the *New Jersey* looked down the barrels of the Japanese six-inch guns across the intervening strip of water and thought: "What if something starts? Whew!"

Regarding liberty for the battleships' crews, the strictest precautions were taken. Roosevelt had instructed Sperry: "Choose only those on which you can absolutely depend. There must be no suspicion of insolence or rudeness on our part. . . . Aside from the loss of a ship I had far rather we were insulted than we insult anybody." Later he added: "If sufficient special first-class men are not available, select first-class men whose records show no evidence of previous indulgence in intoxicating liquor."

As it turned out, there was little cause for apprehension

or restrictions. The Japanese welcome was one vast government-directed, government-controlled production, with nothing left to chance. Policemen and soldiers were told to salute Americans in uniform; merchants were forbidden to raise prices; "*banzais*" were to be shouted on cue and in unison. Thousands of children ("Oh, those children!" marveled Matthews) had been drilled within an inch of their lives to say in English, "Welcome" and "I love you." Tens of thousands of lanterns had been ordered hung on every threshold, each bearing the American colors.

In Yokohama the Japanese gave the Fleet a decorous welcome

Crossed flags were placed in every window, and of like material. If the Japanese flag were silk, the American flag must be of silk. If one were cotton, the other must be cotton. And the American flags correctly carried forty-six stars, acknowledging Oklahoma's admission to the Union, though those on the battleships still carried only forty-five. Since Japanese choral groups had difficulty singing "The Star-Spangled Banner," they applied to the American Embassy for permission to substitute "Columbia, the Gem of the Ocean." Permission was granted.

The people were instructed by printed proclamations on behavior. A few of these instructions, using "foreigners" to denote Americans, were:

Foreigners' dogs shall not be molested by stone throwing or by challenging to fight with other dogs.

No comments or ridicule or mean words shall be given in regard to the dress, bearing or words of foreigners.

Nobody should gaze unnecessarily at foreigners' faces.

Foreigners should not be pointed at with finger.

It shall be borne in mind that foreigners are disgusted with the habit of spitting anywhere and of scattering about the skin of fruit and cigarette ends.

When clearing the teeth or nostrils in the presence of a foreigner, handkerchief shall be used.

The age of a foreigner shall not be asked unless some special necessity demands it.

The 3,000 sailors granted shore leave daily, under the watchful eyes of an augmented shore patrol, behaved impeccably. Each was assigned a Japanese sailor as guide, and every officer had a companion of equal rank. Trains ran continuously between Yokohama and Tokyo, a distance of 18 miles, with tickets free to Americans. In the city, streetcar rides were also free. Though the Japanese had hospitably arranged for free beer to be served by geisha girls, a group of local American missionaries intervened. No beer. No geisha girls. The clean-cut, wholesome American boy much preferred the kind of ice cream served at the Y.M.C.A. The puzzled Japanese switched plans, donned Y.M.C.A. arm bands, and served nothing but ice cream at all events.

Virtually everything offered to the visitors was free. Fruits, cakes, and soft drinks, paper parasols and rickshaw rides were on the town by edict of the mayor—as was admission to the innumerable wrestling matches, geisha dance performances, and juggling acts. Even those not officially conscripted entered into this spirit of largesse. American sailors received a card which many cherished as a souvenir. It read: "Welcome! Welcome! Welcome! American Fleet! Dr. Hasegawa is now very willing to remedy toothache of the crew without charge during her stay in the harbor."

Though relations were friendly there was no unbending. Until one of those small incidents occurred, that so often govern international relations. During an evening fireworks display a rocket set fire to an arch from which a Japanese flag was flying. Three American sailors from the fleet scampered up the burning arch and saved the flag from the flames. From that moment on suspicion changed to warm appreciation. It had been the perfect act to break the ice.

Further warmth was generated when President Roosevelt dispatched an unusually cordial message of greeting to the emperor. The mikado replied with equal cordiality, noting: "The historic relations, the good understanding, and the generous friendship of the United States I count as a valued heritage of my reign." He then issued an order directing the people "to increase in every way possible the enjoyment and pleasure of the American visitors." Reporting this exchange of courtesies, the press in the United States observed, "No two countries ever clasped hands across the sea more closely than on this occasion." A news report from Washington of these events noted that, while a year ago "to send a United States squadron into Japanese waters would be inviting a repetition of the *Maine* affair . . . the enthusiasm that is evidently being shown by the Japanese in welcoming the United States sea fighters is regarded as settling once and for all the reports of friction between this government and that of the Mikado." Rear Admiral Emory wrote from his hotel on October 23: "There should be no doubt regarding the warm feeling the Japanese have for us."

The emperor appeared, unexpectedly, in person at a dinner for the officers in the imperial palace. Admiral Togo also entertained them aboard the battleship *Mikasa,* his flagship during the triumphant war with Russia. Before his departure Admiral Sperry, his coattails and epaulettes flapping, was tossed in a blanket by enthusiastic Japanese marines—to which he responded with a quiet "thank you." The same courtesy of blanket-tossing was extended to Admiral Togo by the American guests. Among them was a young man named "Bull" Halsey who admitted years later that, could he have foreseen the future, he would have let Togo drop.

The Tokyo press had been briefed in advance to throw bouquets at the Americans. "Any newspaper which failed to show proper enthusiasm for the American fleet would be suppressed, fined heavily, or taxed out of existence." Tokyo newspapers, Robert Hart observes, responded with such encomiums as: "The American fleet is a heavenly messenger of peace"; "The Pacific Ocean shall remain for ever pacific"; "Our joy is so great that we cannot contain it"; "The fleet is a cupid joining the hands of the two nations."

American correspondents were not overlooked. Matthews was somewhat taken aback when a geisha schooled him in the use of chopsticks, meanwhile whispering in his ear, "I lof you ver' much." The reporters were each presented with a geisha girl who was thoroughly equipped with government documents stating that she was his official wife for the duration of his visit. None was known to have taken full advantage of the offer.

Somewhat down the bay from main activities a separate celebration was observed around the statue of Matthew C. Perry at Uraga. Americans were joined by venerable Japanese who still remembered the commodore's visit, which had opened Japan to Western trade and commerce. Count Komura, minister of foreign affairs, told the visitors that "he was obliged to confess that Commodore Perry came as an unwelcome guest, but nevertheless had started a new era in the history of Japan. Admiral Sperry now came as a welcome guest, and his advent gave new import to Japan's relations with America, both as regards commerce and good fellowship." Taking this as his cue, Sperry observed that his own name rhymed with Perry, and used the allusion in subsequent speeches, which his fellow Americans found flawless.

When the week was over and the time for *sayonaras* had arrived, the officers of the fleet breathed easier. What had been heralded by jingoists as probable disaster had turned out to be "the greatest prestige triumph of all time." But there were strange international aftermaths to the fleet's reception. As one might have expected, the British were delighted; they had worked upon both nations to effect a happy meeting. The Australians, on the other hand, were horrified; they saw the fleet which they had applauded as an ally now seduced by "Japanese taffy and flapdoodle."

But perhaps the most significant reaction was in Germany, where the kaiser had hoped that the fleet's arrival in the China Sea would spark a cataclysmic war. The emperor, "possessor of the least inhibited tongue in Europe," had gone so far as to announce, not very privately, the formation of a German-American alliance ranged against Japan. Roosevelt had been angered at this premature statement, and now went further in denouncing not only the existence but the probability of such an alliance. The German attitude towards the United States cooled quickly. A few weeks after the visit to Japan, the kaiser ordered a fleet of sixteen battleships to hold maneuvers in the North Atlantic. He would have his own battleship parade, one that might put the American fleet to shame.

Not less significant was the reaction in Japan. When the ceremonial arches had been dismantled and the last flags put away, and while the memory of the Great White Fleet was only three weeks old, the Japanese emperor proclaimed "the greatest naval pageant in all history." A hundred and twenty-three warships, stretching for over twenty miles, made the Great White Fleet's display seem almost insignificant. If Japan had been impressed by the fleet's visit, it had certainly not been intimidated.

10

Disillusionment in China

▶
▶

Poor bewildered and frustrated China. Since the early months of 1908 she had staked her dreams and hopes upon a visit from the Great White Fleet. It was to restore and enhance her position among the powers of the world. It was to reaffirm Roosevelt's Open Door policy, which protected her territorial rights. It was to warn Japan against further intrusion in Manchuria, and underscore the friendly feeling that existed between the United States and China.

But in actual fact, it was to culminate in one of the worst debacles in diplomatic history, compounded by confusion upon error.

Some of the blame could be ascribed to China's own shaky position. The 264-year-old Manchu Dynasty was declining into weakness and corruption. China had allowed herself to be abused and sliced apart. European powers, notably Britain, France, and Russia, had virtually taken possession, by means of "leases," of her harbor cities. Units of foreign navies patrolled her territorial waters; Japan, following the war with Russia, had a tight grip on Manchuria. And what did the dowager empress do? Given a handsome sum from the royal treasury to purchase battleships from Europe, she spent it all on an ivory galleon for the palace lake.

True, Secretary of State John Hay in 1899 had introduced America's Open Door policy "to preserve Chinese territorial and administrative entity . . . and safeguard for the world the principle of equal and impartial trade with all parts of the Chinese empire." But now it looked as if that policy were safeguarding Japan's territorial design on Manchuria while the United States—the only major power free of European alliances and therefore able to come to China's aid—was keeping its eyes averted.

Yes, there was every reason why China looked for some show of strength, some reassurance, from the United States, ideally in the form of a visit from the fleet. But in all this confusion over visits, the Navy Department was frequently at odds with the State Department. One was concerned with naval convenience and expediency, the other with diplomatic interests, and these two considerations often clashed. The Navy Department did not want the fleet to visit China at all. Japan would be enough. Secretary of State Root, sensitive to China's delicate feelings, insisted on the visit and prevailed.

Shanghai was selected as the port of call, and at once the Chinese government—though not pleased with the choice, since Shanghai was overrun with foreigners—began erecting ceremonial arches and pavilions in the city, spending lavishly on decorations. Then the Navy Department announced that Shanghai would not do; its port was too shallow, its channels too tricky.

The next choice settled on Chefu in the Shantung Peninsula. This pleased the Chinese. It was closer to their capital
and closer to German-held bases in Shantung; the Ger-
mans sympathized with China's anti-Japanese resentments.
Admiral Sperry expressed his satisfaction with Chefu, saying that it was possible he and his officers could proceed
from there across the Gulf of Perhilli and up to Peking
"and bow to the Empress." The Chinese government tore
down the arches and pavilions at Shanghai, and once again
began erecting grandstands, arches, and pavilions at Chefu.

Then Washington began to have doubts about Chefu.
It faced the Japanese fortress of Port Arthur and it faced
Korea in which Japan had a major interest. This was no
time to offend the Japanese by honoring an enemy so
close to Japan's spheres of influence. Another port of call
should be selected. Also it would be best to send just half
the fleet, diminishing the importance of the visit, and let
the other half return to the Philippines on the excuse of
needing battle practice. Again the navy suggested cancel-
ling the visit altogether. Root said no. This would be too
great an insult to the Chinese.

Yet another site was settled on, the harbor of Amoy.
Matthews attributed the choice to China on the grounds
that it was "strictly a Chinese port." Actually, China was
shocked and mortified by the selection. Amoy was her
least important port, and far removed from central China
and Peking. Thoroughly disgusted, China began to wonder
if the visit should not best be cancelled altogether. But
Yuan Shih-kai, the dowager empress' first lieutenant, was
insistent. He saw the fleet's appearance as "a giant demon-

stration against Japan." It must take place—even if the site were inauspicious.

Amoy itself wanted "nothing to do with the detestable fleet." It was an independent-minded city, generally opposed to the Manchurian regime. It was also a haven for rebels, anarchists, beachcombers, and coastal pirates. Its only recommendation to the navy was an ample harbor and accessibility. But if the fleet were to be entertained in the vicinity of Amoy a whole new city would have to be built, apart from the existing town, to accommodate them. Amoy itself was far too hostile to the idea of a visit from Americans.

Amoy, in fact, offered no cooperation in the way of supplying building materials and supplies. Accordingly, thousands of coolies and tons of material had to be transported by junk and wagon from the north. The Chinese welcoming committee laid out the planned community on what was known as the parade ground, and the royal treasury, at Yuan Shih-kai's insistence, provided close to half a million dollars for the construction of a "Pleasure City."

The result was something like the pleasure dome of Kubla Khan: a dozen large pavilions with dining tables seating 500 persons each, two Chinese theaters, a sheltered football field and baseball diamond, a permanent building for receiving guests, quarters for the Y.M.C.A., dwellings for visiting dignitaries, storehouses, kitchens, booths for refreshments, stages for outdoor entertainments. Interiors were decorated with satin hangings, ebony furniture, lacquered ornaments and vases, silver bowls and bamboo screens.

All was exquisitely landscaped and dominated by ornamental arches of red, white, yellow, and blue. Shiploads of potted plants were delivered from Canton, with valuable collections of dwarf trees 300 years old. Fleets of river boats brought the living bamboo which was renewed daily. A generating plant was constructed, since Amoy offered no electric lighting, and a railroad built to bring in the supplies. Special docks were erected to receive the launches from the fleet, one for each of the eight battleships.

The dowager empress, refusing to attend herself and allowing none of her higher officials to attend, nevertheless provided $700,000 for entertainment—many times more than any other country had subscribed to entertain the fleet. Hundreds of carriages, mandarin chairs, and rickshaws were brought down from northern cities, 600 servants were provided, actors were imported from Canton and cooks from Shanghai. When it came to food and drink, nothing could be coaxed from nearby Amoy (the New York *Sun* explained to its readers that this was due to cholera raging in that city—a convenient bit of fiction). All had to be brought down, by cart and junk, from Peking or Shanghai.

Security precautions were immense. Two thousand special police were sent down from Peking, who threatened severe punishment to anyone convicted of disorder. These were shortly reinforced by 1,700 regular troops, by which time the armed forces outnumbered any estimated number of expected guests. A high barricade with gun emplacements was built around the Pleasure City, where troops with loaded rifles maintained round-the-clock positions. All "questionable persons" were at once deported from the area, and no one was permitted through the gates without a stringently restricted pass. Pleasure City became an impregnable fortress.

Just as all seemed ready for the fleet's arrival, another of China's inescapable misfortunes struck. The same typhoon that had rocked the fleet in the China Sea on October 12 and 13 now vented its fury on the China coast. With deadly aim, it struck directly at Amoy. Down came the arches and pavilions, all their costly contents buried beneath mud and water. High winds and tides flooded the parade ground to a depth of three feet.

With extraordinary perseverance, Yuan Shih-kai and the committee went back to work. They coaxed another half million dollars from the treasury, brought down more coolies, more materials, and in ten days reconstructed the whole city. Only one thing wouldn't work, the electric generator which had been flooded by the storm. The German cruiser *Niobe,* it so happened, had been standing in the harbor, part of Germany's persistent policy of following the fleet around the globe. One of its electricians repaired the generator, offering further proof to China that the tripartite alliance was in *de facto* operation.

Throughout these ups and downs of fate, a propaganda war had raged between Japan and China. By now Japan had received the fleet, the *whole* fleet, and pointed with derision at the fact that only two divisions—the last two, at that—would visit China. Surely this put China in her place. The dowager empress countered by explaining to her population that half the American fleet had been destroyed in the typhoon; there were only two divisions left.

China joined with Germany in circulating rumors of planned efforts by Japan to sabotage the fleet now in Japanese waters. Japan pooh-poohed these tales as being the anguished outcries of a finally humiliated foe. China was properly insulted by the riposte; a few Peking newspapers were now openly telling their readers that China was receiving the Number Two Fleet and Admiral, while Number One Fleet with Number One Admiral was heading for Manila.

But in general the press was silent on the visit. It is one of the mysteries of the Chinese mind that the nation should go to great efforts to flatter and entertain a foreign guest and then keep its hospitality a secret from the public for fear it might be misinterpreted. An American dispatch from Peking, dated October 31, read: "The presence of the second squadron of the American battleship fleet at Amoy, where the vessels arrived yesterday, is hardly known in Peking. The Chinese newspapers said nothing at all about the visit, and the occurrence is being completely ignored, both officially and otherwise—that is, so far as Peking is concerned."

The communique went on to say: "This silence is the more remarkable because the native press has during the last few weeks given much space to promulgating the idea of an alliance with the United States."

Meanwhile agitators in the city of Amoy began to stir up trouble. Anti-American demonstrations were provoked. Rumors were planted that the Great White Fleet had come to shell and take possession of the city. Hastily 5,000 more troops, this time from the Imperial Guard, were rushed to Pleasure City to strengthen the already formidable forces stationed there. A state of war existed between the two communities.

When Emory anchored his ships off Pleasure City he realized he was facing an explosive situation. No men were allowed ashore at first, and he himself, with his officers, remained on board the *Louisiana* to await developments. No one of truly high importance from the Chinese government was there to greet them. Perhaps the highest-ranking officer was Admiral C. P. Sah of the Imperial Navy—said navy represented by two modest cruisers.

The absence of other officials might be explained by the empress' annoyance and by a news dispatch from Amoy reading: "The revolutionist plot which was unearthed yesterday causes great anxiety, the government officials fearing that its ramifications may be far reaching. The object of the revolutionists is the assassination of high Chinese officials during the reception. Extraordinary precautions are being taken and will continue to be taken during the stay of the fleet here."

Viceroy Sung Chou arrived to represent the province in which Amoy was located, his first official visit to the region. He was promptly threatened with assassination by the revolutionists. Sung took refuge aboard the *Louisiana* where he was joined by other official greeters who found the American flagship safer than their native soil. Meanwhile the government dispatched 3,000 more soldiers from the north, to swell to battle proportions the number of military needing to be fed and housed.

By November 1, Emory considered it safe to send selected groups of men ashore—2,500 making up each days allotment. Approaching Pleasure City through twin rows of armed guards, the sailors were bewildered by this show of force, by the absence of good-natured crowds and customary cheers. Inside, however, they had nothing to object to. All drinks were free, including beer—although an American missionary, there to supervise proceedings, quickly removed beer from the free list. For the first two meals they were served chop suey, after which, with delicate consideration, the Chinese substituted American food. Officers were not so lucky. At the formal reception in the banquet hall they had to submit to such exotic foods as bird nest soup, sharks' fins, rolled fish, and bamboo shoots.

Pleasure City, the men found, was like a vast amusement park without the crowds; only 160 English-speaking Chinese were allowed inside to join the visitors and to act as guides. The sailors ate ice cream, took rickshaw rides, watched magic and acrobatic shows. Baseball and football games were organized among the crews, and the Chinese committee provided gold cups worth $1,200 each for the winners. Silver cups were offered to the winners in field sports and rowing contests. Over these games the armed guards at the barricades kept careful and forbidding watch.

What the Chinese refused to offer in personal friendliness and warmth, they atoned for with expensive gifts, perhaps suggesting that however much Americans might underrate them, they were possessed of riches such as the Americans had rarely seen. Apart from the athletic trophies, each admiral was presented with a silver bowl, and each ship with a larger silver bowl and an ebony-inlaid chair and table set. Officers received lacquer boxes, dressing sets, and ivory jewel boxes. Each enlisted man received a cloisonné cup embossed with the flag of China and Old Glory. The dowager empress unbent enough to send forty wicker crates of fruit to be distributed among fleet personnel.

The dowager empress' birthday took place during the fleet's stay, and Emory appropriately ordered his ships to honor the occasion with a twenty-one-gun salute. Being a diplomat of considerable tact, the admiral then called on the Japanese consulate to explain that since this was also the date of the Japanese emperor's birthday, they could regard the tribute in any way they chose. Emory was also careful to call on the German cruiser *Niobe,* whose electrician had repaired the generating plant, apparently to establish good relations all around.

On the final day, November 4, a fireworks demonstration—the largest in Chinese history—filled the skies with blazing colors. It was more than the Chinese were prepared for or could cope with. Sparks from a rocket set fire to the roof of the Y.M.C.A. building. The fire leaped from roof to roof until Pleasure City was engulfed in flames. Angry Chinese officials accused American sailors of taking advantage of the holocaust to loot the ruined buildings. Admiral Emory hustled his men aboard the ships, and at the crack of dawn the next morning left the harbor.

What was the sum total of this ill-starred pageant? Diligently feeding opiates to his reading public, Franklin Matthews wrote to the *Sun* that "China gave a good old-fashioned handshake to the squadron . . . the welcome was punctilious but none the less from an absolutely open heart . . . she received the squadron with unfeigned gladness; she parted from it with unfeigned regret." Other New York papers published similar effusions. Only two came close to the truth, the *Evening Mail* reporting, "China Not Enthusiastic Over Fleet," while the conservative *Times* headlined, "China Humiliated: Only Half a Fleet."

Looked at even kindly it had been an unrelieved disaster. China had suffered loss of face, the greatest humiliation in the Orient. Japan had been raised, conversely, to unwonted status by its visit from all four divisions of the fleet. The tripartite alliance and German-American alliance, if they had ever been more than gentlemen's agreements, had become apparent myths. President Roosevelt and his professed support of the Open Door had been discredited in Chinese eyes.

Above all, the Chinese government itself was crumbling. This could not be attributed directly to the fleet fiasco. But the latter was another nail pulled from the framework of the throne. The dowager empress and her husband died under mysterious circumstances two weeks after the fleet departed. A week later the Root-Takahira Treaty was announced in Washington. Yuan Shih-kai was thrown out of office. China felt betrayed. Nothing but ruin had descended on her with the visit from the Great White Fleet.

November also marked the conclusion of Admiral Emory's tour of duty with the navy. With what must have been considerable relief, he severed connections with the fleet. His place was taken by Admiral Schroeder from the

Fourth Division, with Schroeder's place filled by the *Vermont*'s captain, William Potter. The *Louisiana* deposited Emory at Hong Kong, then steamed south to rejoin the squadron headed for the Philippines, where Admiral Sperry had arrived with the First and Second Divisions on October 30.

Of the disastrous ending of Pleasure City the American public heard little or nothing. The newspapers were jammed with news of William Howard Taft's election to the presidency over William Jennings Bryan. Taft was a Roosevelt man ("who means well feebly" said the president in confidence) and had been groomed for office by his predecessor. He could be counted on to continue Roosevelt's policy of a strong navy and a strong fleet as essential to America's advanced position in the world.

11

▶

Through the Big Ditch

▶
▶

While the Third and Fourth Divisions were uncomfortably engaged at Amoy, Admiral Sperry took his First and Second Divisions to Subic Bay on Luzon, northwest of Manila, to wait for the other divisions to join him. This they did on November 8 and the entire fleet, relieved to be one again, steamed around the Bataan Peninsula into Manila Bay.

It was Sperry's earnest wish, as it was Manila's, that the city would be free of cholera by now and that his men could go ashore. He knew Roosevelt was anxious to impress the Philippines with both America's naval power and benevolent consideration. He went along with these objectives. But fate still intervened. The epidemic had not subsided; there were even more cases than before. Sperry refused to grant shore leave to any of the men, and kept his vessels well at sea.

The outcry, from the town's American citizens and businessmen, was even greater than during their previous shunning of the city in October. It was no longer disappointment; it was fury. Sperry was openly insulting the

Philippines, lowering American prestige among the natives of the islands, rendering useless the town's preparations to receive the fleet, and denying local merchants their rightful share in the tremendous business accruing from such visits. "Admiral Sperry," wrote the Manila *Times,* "has persisted in a line of conduct boorish and rude to the extreme, and absolutely unwarranted and unpardonable."

For the moment, Sperry was pained but adamant. He knew he was right and he had other things to be concerned with. The principal purpose of the fleet's assembly in the harbor was for battle practice—of even greater importance to the navy than the target drill at Magdalena Bay. For a solid week, from November 10 to 18, the big guns roared in a dramatic and exacting facsimile of war at sea.

Unlike spring target practice, which followed precise guide lines, everything was done to simulate actual battle, its changing circumstances and emergencies. A strategy plan was drawn up in advance, with provisions for unexpected action by the enemy. Canvas targets were shaped to represent, in length and height, the midsection of a hostile warship, and these were positioned as an enemy fleet might be positioned, at distances of one to six miles.

On bugle call, the fleet went into action. Watertight doors around the ships were sealed. Gunners and ammunition crews rushed to their stations. Hospital corps men prepared for casualties in sick bay. The ships raced at full speed towards the enemy. On the order "fire when ready," beam guns and turret guns let loose with all they had, repeating their fire as fast as they could be loaded. There was no pause, no letup in the din and smoke and showers of exploding water blown across the ships. Men fell on cue, and the "wounded" were rushed to sick bay. The guns boomed till the targets were destroyed.

Night practice followed the day's ordeal. This time it was a simulated attack by enemy torpedo boats. The range was closer and the targets smaller. Only the 3-inch guns came into play, lacing into the canvas replicas illuminated by the search-lights. When it was all over, and the ships had come to a halt, the umpires worked on the results, the number of possible casualties, the number of recorded hits. Again the correspondents were forbidden to reveal results, but a later tally showed that—compared with the spring target practice which was merely a rehearsal for the big event—the gunners had showed a 50 per cent improvement in their marksmanship. The hours of shore leave, of being entertained and feted, the months of growing boredom aboard ship, had not impaired the sailors' fighting capabilities.

Even before the battle drill was over, Admiral Sperry received fresh orders from Washington. Roosevelt had been bombarded with letters and wires from Manila demanding that Sperry's orders be countermanded and the city be honored with a formal visit. Roosevelt knew the risk, but he also knew the political and propaganda advantages of yielding to these importunities. The Philippine situation was too touchy to ignore. The city, he told Sperry, must be given the full treatment by the fleet and personnel.

Sperry was outraged, and with justice. The health and welfare of the men were his responsibility. But he'd been overruled. Manila was granted its two days of shore leave, Wild West shows, parades and ceremonies—which nobody wanted save the local merchants, and which Sperry himself avoided. Ironically, a pouring rain dampened the synthetic enthusiasm. At the height of the storm, 1,800 sailors were stranded overnight and housed in churches, schools, and Y.M.C.A. quarters.

At daybreak on December 1, anchors were hoisted and the tired fleet steamed past the rocky island of Corregidor, "the last bit of American soil we should see till we reached our native land." Five days later they passed through the Straits of Singapore, swinging landward to salute that venerable British fortress, then proceeding westward into the fifth sea of their voyage, the Indian Ocean, celebrated in the words and works of Rudyard Kipling. Here the flying fishes played and the nighttime sea broke out in phosphorescent splendor. Perched on the bow turrets of the *Vermont*, a sailor recorded his impressions:

> *The ship drove before her bows two billows of liquid phosphorous and in her wake she was followed by a milky train. As far as the eye reached, the crest of every wave was bright. The fleet seemed to cleave a flood of molten silver, and the sprays which dashed from the bows fell back in glittering showers into the deep.*

In keeping with this mood and atmosphere, the bands aboard ship played the then popular melody, "Glow, little glow worm, glimmer, glimmer. . . ."

On December 13 they sighted the Crown colony of Ceylon. Behind what was then the largest breakwater in the world, the ships made fast to designated buoys. There were no cheering crowds to greet them. At this crossroads of the Indian Ocean, the only deep-water refuge between Singapore and Aden, the natives had seen too many ships and navies come and go to be impressed. Besides, this was not an official visit but a necessary stop for coal. Their reception was courteous, but it had no forced enthusiasm.

There was a week to be spent in coaling and shore leave for the enlisted men. Native divers swarmed about the battleships, pleading for coins to be tossed from deck and bridge. Jewel peddlers arrived by boat to offer, for a few American dollars, "pearls and rubies worth a fortune." One sailor remembered: "The dealers in these 'gems' always had a fantastic tale to go with each stone. The principal story was that it had been stolen from an idol in some far away temple." The same seaman reported an incident when two Indians came on board with two baskets and a flute.

The music from the flute and a few tricks drew quite a crowd around the Indians. With a grand flourish one of the Indians whipped off the cover of a basket. Up shot a cobra and within seconds there was a mad scramble to get away, every man for himself. However, curiosity got the better of the men and with sheepish grins they returned to what they considered a safe distance to watch the show. One of the Indians said that for a pound he would allow a mongoose in the other basket to fight the cobra. When the money was collected the mongoose was released and the cobra dumped out of the basket. After the cobra had made several strikes, the mongoose dispatched it by biting it behind the head.

Ashore the fortune tellers, fakirs, and snake charmers vied for attention. The Ceylonese government provided rail transportation to the colorful mountain city of Kandy, a visit unfortunately marred by fist fights between tars and natives, induced most likely by the heat. Elephants were everywhere among the wildlife, providing transportation, labor power, and amusement. Sailors returned to their ships with monkeys bought at the bazaars. The monkeys promptly climbed to the upper spars and rigging to escape the bears, goats, kangaroos, and other pets aboard.

In fact, the mascot population must have been a trial to the officers by now. A young wireless operator wrote to his family in California:

> There are about forty parrots on board now. They make all kinds of noises. They whistle and squawk and yell. Some of them are getting so they talk a little. They teach them bad words mostly. A sailor's parrot would not make a good impression with "nice" folks. The chief master at arms had a squirrel that would run all over you and was quite cute. I guess he got tired of living for yesterday he jumped overboard. We also have a small deer and a goat and two or three cats. We had a bear but he broke a bottle of liquid fire extinguisher and swallowed some of the glass and he died.

British bewilderment at the American mania for animals to take aboard as mascots was brought out in an incident described by Franklin Matthews. Anxious to own some carved ivory figurines, for which the islanders were famous, Matthews asked a resident where he could buy a

At almost every port, the sailors adopted pets for mascots

string of baby elephants. He was solemnly told that there were plenty of elephants for sale in Kandy, but it was open to question how they'd fare aboard a battleship. What would one do with them? Where would one keep them? In short, old chap, wouldn't it be most awfully awkward?

Before their departure on December 20, Sir Thomas Lipton—who that spring in England had launched the *Shamrock IV*, his latest challenger for the *America*'s Cup— presented the fleet with samples of his tea wrapped in ornamental gift packages, a pound for each sailor, five pounds for the officers, ten pounds for the admirals. It was all they had as gifts for Christmas five days later, apart from token presents passed around halfheartedly. Unlike the same holiday at Trinidad, there was little festivity and little greenery to decorate the ships. Perhaps it was the sense that they were "about as far away from America or American sovereignty as one could get, and it was hot and lonesome." This was not a time to taunt a man with memories of Christmas holidays at home.

Nevertheless, there were sports and games on Christmas Day itself. Sailors were encouraged to duck for silver dollars in buckets filled with water. To make the game more challenging, the dollars were buried in molasses at the bottom of the bucket and concealed with flour. No man came up with more than a mouthful of doughlike flour and molasses, and the dollars were retrieved by hand and passed around as consolation prizes.

New Year's Day was even more subdued, darkened by a telegram from Washington. A severe earthquake, followed by a tidal wave, had wrecked the Sicilian city of Messina and surrounding villages. Casualties were estimated at 150,000 (compared with 452 for the San Francisco earthquake). The ships were told to stand ready for relief work, and Sperry was asked what he could spare in the way of provisions for the stricken city. The admiral offered to dispatch the supply ship *Culgoa* to Messina, which he did; but noted that this would leave the fleet without a future source of food. He requested Washington to send the White Star liner *Liberty,* about to leave New York for Europe, with enough supplies to make up for the loss of the *Culgoa*'s cargo. Two days out, the *Liberty*— carrying 500 tons of fresh and smoked meats, turkeys, potatoes, sugar, eggs, and butter for the fleet—was rammed and sunk by the *Florida* off Nantucket, a catastrophe that Sperry would not learn of until later.

From Colombo to Suez was the second longest and most tiresome stretch of the global voyage. At this point in the cruise there was a sense of both relief and apprehension. They had come two-thirds of the way around the world. The critical visits to Japan and China were behind them. Theoretically they could relax, and rest a bit on the laurels of success. On the other hand, ahead lay the Mediterranean shores of southern Europe. These countries pre- · sented no threat or major problems; but they did have the sophisticated experience of major naval powers. They would not be easily impressed. They would be highly critical of the fleet's appearance and performance.

Had this test come at the earlier stages of the cruise it might have been easier to face. But much had happened in a single year at sea. Not only had vast strides been made in battleship construction—England's *Dreadnought* and other dreadnoughts being built were principal examples—but the ships of the Great White Fleet were growing tired, their sleek hulls barnacle-encrusted and made sluggish with marine growth. Paint could be reapplied and brasswork could be polished; but pipes and boilers were corroded, ropes were worn, plates had been sprung, lifeboats were missing since the China Sea typhoon, and there was a lack of spare parts for repairs. Decidedly the Battle Fleet was not in top form.

Nor were the officers and men. These had been long and grueling months at sea. The first flush of enthusiasm was gone. Sailors were growing restive and homesick. Discipline was harder to maintain, and personal differences were aggravated by confinement. Matters were not helped when, in the Arabian Sea, a sailor from the *Illinois* fell overboard and six of his would-be rescuers were drowned when the lifeboat davits failed from disrepair.

Officers suffered equally from ship fatigue. Jealousies and resentments grew to king size. Irritations were blown up out of all proportions. Damaging rumors found quick circulation. It was whispered that cholera had broken out on such and such a vessel, and it was secretly sailing as a plague ship in their midst. An epidemic of petty thievery broke out, involving food from the galleys and beer from the captain's quarters. Aboard the *Kearsage* these reached such proportions that the captain canceled all shore leaves indefinitely. The crew responded with resentment and restrained rebellion.

Officers looked for scapegoats for their irritation. Aboard the *Georgia,* Admiral Wainwright's flagship, Captain Qualtrough was a favorite target, not entirely without reason. His superior manner and tendency to strut ("He can strut even when sitting down," one officer observed) had won him widespread unpopularity. Wainwright withheld his irritation, but kept his eye on Qualtrough. Someday the captain would slip, and that would be the end of him.

They arrived in the Gulf of Suez two days ahead of schedule, on January 3, 1909, their first landfall of the new year. This was the southern entrance to the 100-mile-long Suez Canal, completed in 1869 by Ferdinand de Lesseps. It was de Lesseps' French-capitalized company which had first struggled with the Panama Canal and finally sold out to the Americans. Unlike Panama, where an intervening mountain range called for the construction of locks, Suez was a water-level route. Nevertheless, navigating its narrow, sinuous length would call for more, if different, skill than traversing the Straits of Magellan.

At Suez a hundred first class seamen from each ship, comprising a party of 1,600, were granted two days leave to visit Cairo and the Pyramids. Blessedly no officers could be spared to make the trip, and the expedition was in charge of a civilian tourist manager. He miscalculated both the number and nature of his charges. Not enough cars had been provided in the train. The men rode happily on platforms, window ledges, and the roofs of cars, shouting and waving at bewildered Bedouins piloting their sheep across the desert. Arriving at Cairo at sundown, the sailors swept like an invading army past the ticket collector to fan out across the city in a jubilant horde. It took the manager until 4 A.M. to round them up and install them in their lodgings.

The dominant color motif of Cairo was the bright red fez of the native male. The following morning 1,600 tasseled fezzes were traded, with high satisfaction on both sides, for 1,600 white caps of the U. S. Navy. Adorned in their new red headgear which contrasted colorfully with blue jackets, the men paraded through the streets of Cairo on lurching donkeys and swaying camels followed by "a beseeching mob of Arabs, Hindus, Hebrews, Greeks, Turks, Nubians, black men, white men, brown men, yellow men, some with long flowing robes, some almost naked, all forcing themselves upon us, having heard no doubt of the 'easy American.'" The city was a "mass of demoralized madmen," wrote Roman J. Miller, but the madness had an infectious gaiety about it.

Many men made the eight-mile trip to the Pyramids at

Gizeh, and rarely did these ancient monuments get such a human going-over. They swarmed over the Sphinx—whose nose had been shot off by Napoleon in 1798 to dishearten military resistance—and were appropriately photographed atop its paws. They climbed the Great Pyramid in dozens, with three husky Bedouin guides apiece to push and wrestle them up the three-foot-high steps. At some slippery point in this ascent it was the strategy of the guides to pause, allow their man to survey the height he clung to, and then settle the matter of a tip—generally to the guides' distinct advantage.

After being photographed again, this time in front of the Pyramid to prove to the folks at home that they had seen this Seventh Wonder of the World, the men returned to Cairo and entrained for Port Said to rejoin their shipmates.

Meanwhile the sixteen battleships had inched their way cautiously through the canal, proceeding in daily groups of four and five and seven. It was the largest fleet ever to pass through the Big Ditch, costing the navy a record $150,000 in tolls. Although the ships were granted a free run, and did not have to pause to let oncoming vessels by, navigation was slow and tricky. In some places the canal was only 120 feet wide. A battleship 75-feet abeam had thus about 20 feet of clearance on each side, not much for a weighty vessel that responded slowly to the helm. Officers were fearful of grounding, recalling the incident of a British warship that had become so firmly stuck that she had had to be blown up to relieve congestion.

Each ship was assigned an Egyptian pilot, but the cap-

tain remained on the bridge to assume responsibility, stay-
ing there for the eighteen hours required to complete the
passage. On the bridge of the *Georgia,* Wainwright's flagship, the admiral looked over Captain Qualtrough's shoulder with critical apprehension. Undoubtedly this did nothing to relieve a natural nervousness on Qualtrough's part.
An error in orders, an accident to the steering mechanism,
would send the ship aground. And indeed, whatever the
cause, the *Georgia* lurched to a shuddering halt when a
third of the way through. Qualtrough called for reversed
engines; the propellers churned up billows of foam but the
ship remained stuck, its lengthy ram buried solidly in mud.
While the vessels behind the *Georgia* waited, tugs were
rushed to the scene and camels brought by land, and both
worked for ninety minutes to loosen the great battlewagon
from the mire and send it finally upon its way. Wainwright
said nothing, but Qualtrough's status moved another notch
down.

By the end of three days the last of the ships had passed
through the canal. In charge of the forward searchlight on
the *Connecticut,* Carroll Morgan claimed the title of "First
Man Through the Big Ditch." The fleet tied up to buoys
at Port Said. No men were allowed leave at Port Said, the
"Wickedest City in the World," but correspondent Matthews went ashore to see if it deserved its reputation. He
found it did. "From five hundred to one thousand men
lurk in the shadows of night—they call themselves guides—
and they dash to your side and whisper things in your ear
that make you clench your fists." Matthews sought refuge
in a hotel till it was time to go back to the *Louisiana.*

The men themselves showed no great eagerness to get ashore. It was time for coaling ship again, and for once they did not begrudge the task. The fleet was on the home stretch now, and anything that would speed it on its way was unobjectionable. It was here, at this "wickedest spot" on earth, that the men made the acquaintance of a character calling himself "Holy Joe." He arrived alongside the ship in a rowboat. He was selling sand and broken pieces of stone with the cry,

> *Holy Joe from the Holy Land*
> *Sells holy stones and holy sand.*

For ninety-odd miles along the Suez Canal there is nothing but sand and stone.

Aboard the *Connecticut* during this layover, Admiral Sperry had a troublesome assignment. It was the matter of protocol and schedules for their remaining month in foreign waters. As with the cruise around South America, invitations had been pouring in from European and Mediterranean countries, all demanding a visit from the fleet. It was the penalty of their success. In the eyes of the world the cruise had been transformed from an ill-advised stunt to a naval triumph. Even the diffident British had been moved to praise. Printed the London *Times,* "We in England can have nothing but admiration for so big a thing as this cruise has proved to be."

There were matters of national contingencies to be considered. Turkey was on the brink of war with Austria-Hungary over the latter's annexation of Bosnia. Turkey needed some show of American support. France had welcomed Roosevelt's judgment at the Algeciras Conference, and now hoped for a Franco-American-British alliance that would "insure the peace of the world." So France deserved attention. Italy had been rocked by the earthquake at Messina. This would call for special action yet to be determined. Spain of course could be passed by; she had been wiped off the map by Dewey at Manila.

How could Sperry call at important ports of all these countries and still be back at Hampton Roads on February 22, the date set for his return? Only one expedient was possible. He would split the fleet up into separate units and assign each a portion of the harbors to be touched at. The relative importance of the visiting battleships would be roughly matched with the importance of their hosts. On paper the itinerary might work out like this:

First Division:
Italy (Naples, Genoa), France (Villefranche).

Second Division:
France (Marseilles) and Tangier.

Third Division:
Turkey (Smyrna), Lebanon (Beirut), Greece (Athens, Salonika).

Fourth Division:
North Africa (Tripoli), Malta, and Algiers.

All Divisions:
Missions accomplished, assemble at Gibraltar.

With more than a dozen ports to call at, including Gibraltar where the fleet would reunite, no whole division could remain intact. Single ships, or groups of two and three, would sometimes have to do the honors. And there was the problem of the earthquake at Messina. How many ships would have to be diverted for relief work? Sperry kept his itinerary flexible, to meet each situation as it came along.

One thing was working in his favor as he approached this international "parade ground of the world." Because of the Messina tragedy there would be no formal welcomes, no staged pageantry to consume the time and exhausted energies of officers and personnel. Ceremonies would be limited to official calls and courtesies. At this stage of the game, it was something to be thankful for.

12

Mediterranean Salmagundi

As the Great White Fleet steamed out of Port Said into the calm blue of the Mediterranean, it entered a whole new theater of diplomacy and jockeying for power. Half its cruise had been spent among the countries of the New World, young, jealous, struggling for recognition, but admittedly secondary to the United States in military and economic development. That part of the cruise had been a parade of power, a show of brotherly concern for lesser neighbors.

The second half of the cruise had been concerned with the delicate matter of soliciting support from Australasia and Hawaii and the Philippines, and welding a united front against Japan—at the same time holding out for the integrity of China. The cruise had been not so much a parade of force as an exercise in diplomacy. Its goal had been peace in the Pacific, resistance to Japanese expansion, and the establishment of the United States as a two-ocean power.

Now the fleet entered the troubled waters of the Old World. Peace prevailed, but it was a shaky, frightened peace. Austria-Hungary was stirring up trouble in the Balkans; she and Germany sought to dominate the Continent. Great Britain, once the stable, order-keeping, master power of the world, was having her position challenged by a growing German navy. Russia was recovering from her war against Japan, and threatening the German-Austrian alliance on the latter's eastern flank. Italy was linked to that alliance, but tottering in indecision. France was on England's side, but more out of fear than sympathy, caught in the middle as it were. Spain hardly counted any more; England's Gibraltar was all that was left of military might on Spanish soil.

In all this froth of strained alliances and shifting power, only one unpleasant truth emerged. War between Germany and England was inevitable. If temporarily avoided, it remained inevitable. The question was when, and how, the dominoes would fall.

The United States wanted no part of these alliances and intrigues. But Roosevelt had brought the nation to an awareness of its new role in the world. It could not float in comfortable isolation. From now on it would have to play, to some extent, the European game. It would have to choose its friends and base its actions on that choice. It would have to stay powerful but uncommitted—ready to jump to the side that it considered morally right as well as politically expedient.

This was the most difficult of all roles. It called for mature and seasoned statesmanship. The United States was emerging from its Age of Innocence into an age of international, astute diplomacy. Maybe it was high time. But it put the Great White Fleet in an anachronous position. For the fleet was a product of that Age of Innocence. It was a floating symbol of Independence Day orations, of Old Glory flying over village greens, of New England apple pie and Casey at the bat and a good five cent cigar. If anything gave it importance in the eyes of Europe it was not the number of its guns or the ammunition in its magazines. It was what it stood for in the way of stable democratic government in an unstable world. It was the rugged, enviable stature of its people. This was a new criterion to measure up to.

Sperry might have wished that this test had come earlier, when the fleet was fresh and the men enthusiastic. He was working now with tired tools, and he himself was tired. It was not the best thing in the world to split the fleet up at this time, sending it off on separate missions under separate commands. It broadened the field of possible mistakes. But he had no choice. In a month it would be over, and he kept his fingers crossed.

A map of the Mediterranean countries as appearing, say, in the *Oxford University Press Atlas* for 1914 (or any atlas of about that time) shows a much different picture than such a map today. It explains some of the now confusing names and nationalities in the fleet's log. Salonika, Beirut, and Tripoli, for example, then belonged to Turkey and not to Greece, Lebanon, and Libya. Algiers was still a part of metropolitan France. Tangier was a disputed protectorate of France and Spain. The Balkan countries, while outside the fleet's itinerary, were about to undergo complete revision. The Great White Fleet was glimpsing, for the last time, a world and a civilization that would never be the same again.

The sixteen battleships split up on their separate Mediterranean missions on January 6, signaling good-bye to one another with the mute regret of a closely knit family parting with its members. Sperry took his First Division northwest towards the boot of Italy and three days later entered the Straits of Messina. The straits had been so badly churned by the tidal wave and earthquake that the ships moved cautiously, checking the buoys against their own soundings, shocked to see the verdant, classic countryside dissolve into the charred and ruined suburbs of the city.

Messina itself was a total wreck, its waterfront and leveled streets cluttered with rubble over which lone figures roamed like vultures. Beneath the rubble lay the unrecovered bodies of a host of dead. In fact, the Sicilian city was such an unregenerated burial heap that cold but realistic government officials had suggested it be covered over with a coat of quicklime and left to its consumption.

Following orders, the provision ship *Culgoa* was standing by in the harbor, still ferrying food and medical supplies to those on land. Sperry ordered the squadron to anchor while he went ashore to reconnoiter and see how his battleships might be of use. He was met by the American ambassador to Italy, Lloyd Griscom, who was heading up American relief work on the island. Griscom gave him the surprising news that his ships were as welcome as the plague. Italy resented what it regarded as "American interference" in a personal, internal tragedy. The king considered it presumptuous to assume that Italy was too poor or too unequipped to care for its own victims of disaster. Griscom suggested that Sperry remove his squadron before giving more offense.

Sperry did so by sending the *Minnesota, Vermont,* and *Kansas* on to Villefranche. But while he was in earshot of the suffering and starving, he could not bring himself to remove the *Culgoa* from her task of mercy, nor could he himself leave Italy without a face-to-face encounter with his irrational host.

The *Connecticut* sailed on to Naples where Sperry entrained for Rome and managed an audience with Victor Emmanuel III. The king would not discuss the matter of assistance to Messina, and offered no invitation to the fleet to stay or visit Genoa as planned. He did, however, warm to a discussion of battleships, and spent most of Sperry's time in lauding the Italian navy. At the end of the interview, the disheartened Sperry went back to his ship and sailed to rejoin the rest of his division.

Villefranche, not far from Nice, was then one of the smarter resorts of the French Riviera, an attractive half-moon harbor with a terraced backdrop of pink villas. Although by agreement there were to be no reception ceremonies, balls, or banquets—out of deference to mourning Italy—French *joie de vivre* found a way to sugarcoat this edict. It was the only port in which any units of the Great White Fleet found civilized and generous entertainment till they reached Gibraltar.

The First Division rested at Villefranche for nearly two weeks, during which the men were granted leave to visit Paris, Switzerland, Rome, or any goal their funds allowed.

Those remaining with their ships, primarily the officers, were entertained by American society matrons who had come there for the season. In fact the presence of the four white battleships, with their handsome officers who knew the latest dance steps, marked the season with distinct success. Reginald MacKenna, first lord of the British admiralty, entertained the visitors aboard his yacht *Enchantress*. Sperry was driven by American Ambassador Henry White to the Nice casino where he lost heavily at roulette, concluding that the casino and the resort itself were "vulgar and ostentatious." By January 27 the men were rounded up from the interior and the squadron sailed for its Gibraltar rendezvous.

With the Second Division, Admiral Wainwright sailed directly to Marseilles. "Far out at sea," remembered S. P. Smith of the Nebraska, "we had a sandstorm that relieved us having to sand our decks to scrub them." Smith also remembered, without much revulsion, eating "plenty of horsemeat" on arrival in Marseilles. "In the markets you could see the quarters of horses hanging with hooves not taken off."

Their reception in France's largest port and second largest city was raucous and enthusiastic. They were surrounded in the harbor by French warships, and on land by Frenchmen eager to talk battleships and navy. Admiral Wainwright was all but kidnapped and taken to Toulon to witness the launching of France's first of sixteen dreadnoughts, the *Voltaire*. Somewhat as had the Australians, the French seemed anxious to regard the visit in terms of American support against a common threat, in this case

The U.S.S. Connecticut *under way*

Germany. They talked of alliance with Great Britain and America. They rationalized figures just released—showing the United States and Germany with 31 battleships apiece —as putting the United States in second place among the navies of the world. The United States fleet weighed 35,000 tons more than the German fleet.

Wainwright finally broke away from this excessive hospitality, sent the *New Jersey* and *Rhode Island* to Gibraltar, and sailed south with the *Georgia* and *Nebraska* to Tangier. The purpose of this fractured visit was to show support for Roosevelt's decision at the Algeciras conference that Morocco fell rightfully in France's sphere of influence. To this end it was important to impress the present anti-German sultan, Moulay Hafid, with American good will. Thus a reception was arranged for all concerned at the Ville de France Hotel.

The reception was Captain Qualtrough's long-anticipated downfall. He was seen staggering in the hall and clinging to a pillar for support. Admiral Wainwright promptly arrested him for drunkenness on duty, and subsequently called for his court-martial. The trial was held three days later at Gibraltar. Qualtrough protested that he had been on the bridge of his ship till midnight on the eve of the party, had been up at 4 A.M., and had had nothing but black coffee all day long. At the reception he had had one glass of sherry and a strong cigar and these had disagreed with him.

Qualtrough's defense was accepted and he was acquitted by the court. But not by Admiral Sperry, who reversed the decision and sent Qualtrough home a prisoner on his own ship. The case roused a storm of debate, pro and con, in the United States, enlivened by the revelation that eleven other officers had been charged with drunkenness on the cruise. The furor led to no conclusion apart from the fact that diplomatic partying and obligatory toasts were heady pitfalls for a naval officer.

To save precious time before the fleet was due to leave for home, Rear Admiral Seaton Schroeder split in two his Third Division, sending the *Missouri* and *Ohio* to Piraeus, the Greek port for Athens. He himself with the *Louisiana* and *Virginia* sailed for the Turkish cities of Beirut and Smyrna. Beirut greeted them, as had Manila, with the threat of plague. The city was quarantined. Schroeder was advised to leave at once, and did so, sailing to the Aegean port of Smyrna.

Here he was confronted with a delicate diplomatic problem common to the cruise. This was the use of the fleet's presence to promote the nationalistic interests of its hosts. As a result of Austria's annexation of Bosnia, Turkey was on the brink of war with the Grand Alliance—Austria, Germany, and Italy. Crucial to such a war would be the Dardanelles, the passage between the Black Sea and the Mediterranean, over which looked Turkish Constantinople. Now Turkey's naval minister, Arif Pasha, suggested that the fleet should visit Constantinople where, he told Franklin Matthews, "we shall attempt to entertain the visitors with fetes comparable to those arranged for them in Japan, Australia and New Zealand."

Schroeder was reluctant to fall into this trap. The straits had been closed for years to foreign battleships. Even though Turkey now relaxed this policy, and both England and America might favor such a visit, it would be too obviously taking sides with Turkey in her current quarrel. Schroeder refused the invitation but went as far as possible to court good will, even inviting ten eager young Turks to return home with him for a naval education in America.

The threat of war was happily removed when Austria offered Turkey cash for the acquisition of Bosnia. Simultaneous with this event, a series of tremors shook the eastern Mediterranean coast. The battleships trembled at their moorings, and ashore the buildings shook and crumbled. Smyrna was in a state of panic, and all festivities were cancelled. Schroeder kept his men aboard for the three days that the quakes continued.

Meanwhile the *Missouri* and *Ohio* had stopped at Athens, where the officers flattered the Greek King George on his miniscule navy and the sailors visited the Parthenon, then on to Salonika for a three-day celebration in their honor. On January 20 they joined the rest of the squadron at Smyrna, and all four ships sailed westward for Gibraltar.

Admiral William Potter's Fourth Division had been assigned the less important ports of Africa, plus the fortified British base of Malta. Potter sent the *Kentucky* to the Turkish port of Tripoli—citadel in America's war with the piratical Barbary States a hundred years before—on the American consul's recommendation that "I am a firm believer in the efficacy of 'showing the flag' in cities such as this one." Tripoli, however, was of secondary importance to the Turkish ports on the Third Division's itinerary. One battleship would be enough for her. Meanwhile Potter sailed with the *Wisconsin, Kearsage,* and *Illinois* towards Malta. They were approaching the British island when a message from Sperry ordered that the *Illinois* be sent to Messina to seek and recover the bodies of the American Consul Arthur S. Cheney and his wife.

Every sailor with the Great White Fleet had his particular memories of the global voyage. Those of Ray Lavalette and Robert McKnight of the *Illinois* were of searching through the rubble of Messina, beneath which lay thousands of the earthquake's dead. Four hundred sailors from the ship were sent ashore and armed with picks and shovels to dig in the wreckage of the consulate, watched suspiciously by vultures, looters, and ghost-like survivors. After five hours the bodies of the Cheneys were recovered, and carried in wooden coffins to the *Culgoa* for shipment to America. Its mission completed, the *Illinois* joined the rest of her division at Malta.

There was marked contrast between the squadron's reception at Malta and that at Trinidad the year before. They came now not as "tramps" to be ignored, but as victors to be catered to. Whatever the British may secretly have thought about the battleships, in view of their superior *Dreadnought,* they went all out to lavish praise on Potter's squadron. No less than five British battleships were there to greet them, along with the duke of Connaught, brother of King Edward VII. Not only that, but the Admiralty's Sir Reginald McKenna sailed his *Enchantress* from Villefranche to join with Potter in reviewing the combined British-American fleet.

There were sound reasons for this change in British attitude toward the visitors. Seemingly peaceful and prosperous on the outside, Europe was a smouldering tinderbox within, girded to the teeth for war. No one felt that the tongue-loose kaiser, plagued with envy and suspicion of his neighbors, could be kept at bay for long. The Triple Entente of England, France, and Russia could well use another ally on the high seas. Time postponed but did not falsify their hopes. The war they dreaded would break out in 1914, five years distant. Three years later the United States would be involved, and on their side.

When the *Kentucky* returned from Tripoli, the Fourth Division moved briefly to Algiers. Briefly, because once given shore leave the crews headed for the legendary Casbah where they clashed head on with the Algerian police. The latter took a band of sailors into custody, only to be attacked by another contingent of Americans who fought successfully for their release. The Yankee tars then headed for the harbor, jumped aboard a waiting launch, and rammed into a native boat that accidentally crossed their path. Wisely, Admiral Potter left Algiers two days ahead of schedule, and headed northwest towards Gibraltar.

On approaching Gibraltar, January 31, neophytes with the cruise—and they were many—were told to watch for the sign "Prudential has the strength of Gibraltar" which they had seen pictured on the great rock's face. Those who first sighted it would receive free shares of stock in the Prudential Life Insurance Company. This kept the men at the rails until they found themselves inside the harbor, deprived of any claim on life insurance stock.

As at Malta the British welcomed them with open arms. Since it was Sunday no salutes were fired, but Vice-Admiral James E. G. Goodrich, in command of the entire military complex of Gibraltar, called at once on Admiral Sperry on the *Connecticut* without waiting for the latter to call first on him. The American squadrons, arriving separately from their various assignments in the Mediterranean, were surrounded by warships of the British, French, Dutch, and Russian fleets. The following morning, when the appropriate salutes were indicated, "it seemed as if the navies of half the world had united in an assault upon the historic fortress." The playing of five national anthems simultaneously by the ships' bands led to an equally unusual cacophony, which one officer described as "musical pandemonium."

A signalman aboard the *New Jersey* remembers: "At Gibraltar we anchored fairly close to several Russian men-of-war. We saw the brutality of the Russian officers, beating their men with swagger sticks on several occasions. One day one of the Russian ships, the *Osysilyaba,* proceeded to sea about three miles in order to hang a man, one of their crew. We knew it took place but could not get details. The information we had came from a signalman on a British man-of-war who semaphored that the Russian captain had requested permission to perform the hanging in port but was refused by the British commander of the port."

There was much to do at Gibraltar besides the customary banquets and receptions for the officers and sightseeing by the sailors. Two days were spent in coaling, interrupted by the visitors from shore. There was Captain Qualtrough's trial, presided over by Admiral Schroeder with his fellow officers making up the court. And there was the critical matter of food. Sperry had learned by now of the *Liberty*'s loss at sea with its cargo of provisions for the fleet. Having donated the *Culgoa*'s supplies to the stricken survivors of Messina, the fleet itself was dangerously short of food.

To forestall the prospect of famine aboard the ships, the fleet's paymaster was dispatched to Marseilles to purchase $150,000 of meat. The meat arrived via the *Culgoa* but was found on inspection to be contaminated. As a result, Sperry faced perhaps the most serious crisis of the cruise. Disaster was averted, however, when the British garrisons at Gibraltar proferred stores of bully beef and hardtack which, carefully rationed, would see the battleships back to Hampton Roads.

13

Time of Reckoning

The weather was misty and overcast at Gibraltar as, on the morning of February 6, 1909, a stream of multi-colored signal flags on the *Connecticut* relayed the order to be under way, and again the great chains rattled in the hawseholes. It was the last time the white ships would hoist anchor in a foreign harbor. "The difficult operation of getting the battleships out of the narrow war basin of the port," wrote the *Times* correspondent, "was skilfully accomplished under the critical eyes of the foreign naval officers afloat and ashore."

Customarily no salutes were fired on departure, but Admiral Goodrich's flagship *Devonshire* took up position at the harbor's entrance and hoisted and saluted the American flag as the Great White Fleet passed out to sea. On the *Connecticut* the band played "God Save the King," and Goodrich's men responded with "The Star-Spangled Banner." Down the succeeding line of ships the musicians raised the strains of "Home, Sweet Home" as the vessels in Indian file proceeded through the straits and headed for the Chesapeake, two thousand miles away.

Below decks the ships' tailors went to work on the "Homeward Bound" pennants, 150 to 175 feet long, to be strung from the main trunks on entering Hampton Roads. It was their happiest assignment of the voyage and they worked, wrote Captain Roman Miller, "with a fervor as great as that of Betsy Ross when she made the first Stars and Stripes in 1776." At the conclusion of the voyage, many of the pennants were destined to be cut up and distributed as souvenirs.

With their departure the barometer began to drop, and two days out the sea took on the angry face of an Atlantic winter. Those who had looked for a pleasant and relaxing homeward trip spent sleepless nights of watch on pitching decks, peering vainly across mountainous seas for some glimpse of their fellow ships. The voyage was "one of continuous horror," wrote Robert E. Coontz, executive officer of the *Nebraska*. "Boats were carried away, men were washed overboard, and things were most discouraging to the officers who wanted the vessels to look their best upon reaching Hampton Roads."

It was the worst series of storms since the typhoon in the China Sea. No one was allowed on the forecastles, which were awash with foaming brine. "At times," wrote a sailor in his private log, "our stern would rise so high out of water that the huge propellers would strike space, for an instant shaking the ship from stem to stern, and the stern going down would send a white curling trail backwards that hissed and roared like Niagara Falls."

Aboard the *Vermont,* as on the other ships, the mess halls were a shambles. It was useless to use the dining tables, and the customary jokes about "Duke's Mixture," applying to the refuse on the floors, were skipped. The sailors ate sitting on the floor cross-legged, propped against the walls, their dispositions not improved by the British bully beef and hardtack.

In midocean, Sperry received a message from the mainland, something of a record for the newly instituted wireless, informing him that they would be met at sea by the third or "home" squadron of Admiral Conway H. Arnold's Atlantic Fleet, consisting of four battleships and five cruisers. These would act as escorts to accompany the Great White Fleet to its reception at Hampton Roads.

On the morning of the seventeenth the vanguard of these ships was sighted, the battleships *Maine, New Hampshire, Idaho,* and *Mississippi,* and the scout cruiser, *Salem.* The gray war paint contrasted drably with the white of Sperry's vessels, but the new-type basket masts of the *Idaho* and *Mississippi,* "resembling huge oil towers," were a trademark of the great ships of the future. There was no letup in the intermittent high seas, and that night the *New Hampshire* provided excitement with the signal for man overboard. Searchlights were trained on the angry waters in a vain attempt to recover the lost seaman, A. J. Haft.

The following day they were met by the remaining units of Arnold's fleet, the new armored cruisers *North Carolina* and *Montana,* and scout cruisers *Birmingham* and *Chester.* Now the Sweet Sixteen was the "Big Twenty-five" as they swept towards home on the last leg of the voyage. In spite of the weather, they were hours ahead of schedule and on February 21 Admiral Sperry ordered the fleet to anchor off Fort Henry while a last coat of white paint was applied to the badly battered hulls, leaving only a telltale streak of green at the waterline where the fouling of marine growth started. That night Captain Miller strolled the deck of the *Vermont* "to note the effect of home-coming." He wrote:

> *Needless to say, everywhere was evidence of intense pleasure, and impatience as intense. Here were the boys of the whole people, north and south, united in the interests of the whole republic and now homeward bound. They had come from the Florida everglades, from the golden-gated Pacific, from the farms of our mighty West, and the shores of our inland seas. They had come from the Atlantic border, from Pennsylvania, New York, Tennessee, and Kentucky, from New England, from Alabama, from Georgia, from Texas, and all were now dreaming of home. Songs! Never have I heard a more enthusiastic mingling of national, sentimental, and comic songs blended in one hopeless mass of melody. . . .*

Sperry had finally refused to receive any of the hundreds, if not thousands, of messages pouring in by wireless from navy wives and sweethearts. After perusing one which read, "Cheer up, ducky darling, I'll be waiting for you at the dock," he concluded that too many of these would clutter up communications. While he was declared a "heartless brute" by those on shore, it did not diminish the crowds which swarmed over the Chamberlin Hotel in a competitive fever to be the first to sight the fleet. The waters off Norfolk and Old Point Comfort were crowded with excursion steamers from Baltimore and Richmond, as well as countless pleasure craft waiting suspensefully in the mist. The *New York Times* reported "Navy-mad Throngs at Hampton Roads" for the commencement of "fleet week."

The following morning, Washington's Birthday, the sun

should have shown brightly for their arrival. But the weather remained overcast. The President's yacht, *Mayflower*, took up its position near Fort Henry as Admiral Sperry's Battle Fleet, at the head of a naval column seven miles long, passed in review. As each ship passed the *Mayflower*, a salute of twenty-one guns was given, consuming more gunpowder than at the Battle of Manila. With twenty battleships in the line, including Admiral Arnold's four, the New York press was able to label the review "the greatest naval pageant in American history."

On the deck of the *Mayflower* Roosevelt's eyes were misty with a pardonable pride. "Do you remember the prophecies of disaster?" he asked those beside him. "Well, here they are!"—and he pointed to the ships returning after fourteen months without a scratch. "Isn't it magnificent?" "It was the apotheosis of Roosevelt," wrote the *New York Times,* "the one supreme magnificent moment in the career of a man who more than any other made possible this review of the biggest aggregate of splendid warships that has been ever gathered under one flag."

When the ships dropped anchor, the president did not wait for the four admirals to come to him. He made his way to the *Connecticut* (and later to the other flagships) to greet its admiral and crew in person. In his haste to climb the forward turret he fell and had to be assisted, but once aloft his words came genuinely from the heart:

Admiral Sperry, officers, and men of the battle fleet: Over a year has passed since you steamed out of this harbor and over the world's rim, and this morning the hearts of all who saw you filled with pride as the hulls of the mighty warships lifted above the horizon. . . . This is the first battle fleet that has ever circumnavigated the globe. Those who perform the feat again can but follow in your footsteps. . . . You have falsified the predictions of the prophets of failure. In all your long cruise not an accident worthy of mention has happened to a single battleship. . . . As a war machine, the fleet comes back in better shape than it went out. In addition, you, the officers and men have shown yourselves the best possible ambassadors and heralds of peace. . . . We welcome you home to the country whose good repute among nations has been raised by what you have done.

Tirelessly the president repeated his greeting aboard the flagships *Georgia, Louisiana,* and *Wisconsin,* and then gathered the admirals in the cabin of his *Mayflower* to declare, "Not until some American fleet returns victorious from a great sea battle will there be another such homecoming, another such sight as this. I drink to the American Navy!" It was perhaps the last toast of his final term as president. In barely more than a week he would leave the White House in the hands of William Howard Taft, confident that he would have a man in office who would carry out his aspirations for a greater navy.

Almost before the cheering and the sounds of greeting died, yard workers from the naval base began chipping off the ornate sculpture of the vessels' prows, and painting the hulls a somber, battle gray. For the days of pageantry and pomp were over. It was time to return to the prosaic world of harsh reality. Time, perhaps, to ask: What did it all amount to? What was the ultimate significance of this historic voyage?

When the Fleet returned to Hampton Roads in 1909, Roosevelt boarded each of the four flagships to deliver his speech of welcome and congratulations. Admiral Sperry received the president aboard the Connecticut

To the fourteen thousand sailors scattering now towards their homes, the answer was relatively easy. They might have griped throughout the voyage, and professed a longing to be anywhere but on the high seas. But almost to a man—as their surviving letters indicate—they regarded it in retrospect as "the adventure of a lifetime." "It was a never-to-be-forgotten experience, for which I am most grateful." "A wonderful trip, that keeps coming back to me in memory." "It would cost any individual person many thousands of dollars to make such a cruise and be entertained as we were by foreign governments."

To the officers it had been a less unmitigated triumph. Their responsibilities while under way had been severe, their social obligations while ashore had been demanding. Many had been tripped up by the combination. But those who had survived these trials had profited from the experience and been promoted. One was Admiral Thomas C. Kincaid, executive officer on the *Nebraska,* who commanded the Seventh Fleet in the Pacific naval victories of World War II. Another was Admiral William B. Halsey who, as commander of the Third Fleet, paced MacArthur's reconquest of the Philippines in 1944. Yet another, Fleet Admiral Ernest J. King who commanded in the Pacific during 1941–45. And another still, Captain George A. Alexander, commander of the battleship *Arizona* during the bombing of Pearl Harbor, who wrote in the summer of 1968, "That great cruise made a real naval officer out of me."

Regardless of all other considerations, the voyage had been a "superb technical achievement," as Robert Hart observes, setting numerous world records:

Theirs was the largest fleet ever to accomplish a circumnavigation. It had traveled farther (forty-six thousand miles), with unparalleled endurance (four hundred and thirty-four days), touched the equator five times, visited more continents (six) and more countries (twenty-six) than any other navy on a single cruise. It had carried more men (fourteen thousand), consumed more coal (four hundred and thirty-five thousand tons at a cost of $1,967,553), worn out more shovels (an average of two hundred and fifty on each ship), and burned in the neighborhood of one hundred thousand rounds of saluting powder, about thirty times the amount expended in the Spanish-American War.

From the standpoint of the navy, the voyage had been revealing and instructive, and not unduly costly. Only $1,619,834 had been spent on the cruise above the normal cost of maintaining sixteen battleships at home. Even before he arrived at Hampton Roads, Admiral Sperry had summarized his conclusions. "This cruise marks an epoch in our naval annals, for the fleet has found itself welded into a unity. . . . The American people have come to appreciate the importance of sea power in the preservation of a just peace. . . . Enlistments in the Navy will certainly be stimulated by the general interest in this cruise and the splendid opportunities afforded the men to see the world."

Sperry estimated that the entire fleet could go half the distance again without drydocking for repairs. He was supported in this by ex-Secretary Metcalf who observed, "the cold facts are that the ships have practically taken care of their own repairs on this cruise." In these publicized summations, "Fighting Bob" Evans was strangely silent. Perhaps embittered by the fate which had prevented his completing the voyage, he had swung over to the side of the skeptics, and now even supported Henry Reuterdahl's findings that the ships and navy needed overhauling. Evans was not with Roosevelt to greet the returning fleet at Hampton Roads.

Discipline throughout the cruise had generally been excellent, all things considered. There had been desertions, but over all, these had not exceeded the average number experienced in any similar period. There had been fourteen courts-martial for drunkenness and conduct unbecoming a gentleman, with twelve convictions—again not above normal. Illness and deaths were what would have been expected in home waters. Outstanding on the positive side was the excellent performance of the gunners at Magdalena Bay and Manila. The men were found to "shoot straighter with the six- and twelve-inch guns than any other men in the world." Sperry was undoubtedly right in asserting that "the high class of the enlisted personnel has perhaps had as much as anything to do with advertising the formidability of the fleet abroad."

In Theodore Roosevelt's *Autobiography* he notes: "My prime purpose was to impress the American people; and this purpose was fully achieved. . . . No single thing in the history of the United States Navy has done as much to stimulate popular interest and belief in it as the world cruise."

The American public had been thoroughly enchanted. Uncle Sam's Greatest Show on Earth had played to an enthusiastic and applauding gallery, concerned with little more than style and flair—and the fleet had provided them with style and flair. Souvenir books and pictures of the ships and admirals sold incredibly. Men and women sported boaters with naval decorated hatbands. Children dressed like the jack tars on the packages of Crackerjack. Models of the battleships appeared in merchants' windows and for sale on counters. Souvenirs distributed by the returning seamen were cherished sentimentally by families and sweethearts.

Not all were equally enthusiastic. *Leslie's Weekly* for February 4, 1909, observed: "The whole world has probably been laughing in its sleeve over our great battleship fleet cruise. The vessels themselves and the crews are worthy of all admiration, but it is an appalling fact that for months they have been at the mercy of unarmed ships which accompanied them—27 coal ships, all of them foreign, not one of them American. The fleet was thus almost wholly dependent on alien craft for its needed fuel."

The criticism was just, but the faults could be corrected. Almost every officer on the cruise had come to recognize that an effective navy must have its own colliers, and must be able to rely upon sufficient offshore yards and bases built strategically around the world. Pearl Harbor and Guantanamo were significant starts in this direction, and more would develop in succeeding years.

From a world standpoint, from the view of America's international position, the results were mixed. The cruise had won the respect of many and the enmity of some. It would take China years of patient wooing to recover from her injured feelings. German-American relations, which had started off well and then deteriorated, would never be the same again. South American countries had been duly impressed, sometimes resentfully envious, but generally grateful that a mighty power was concerned with their integrity. The Monroe Doctrine had been given teeth.

In his excellent history, *The United States and World Sea Power,* Elmer Potter notes: "In every way the cruise was an unqualified success. . . . in the Antipodes and in Middle Eastern and European ports of call, the fleet was hailed as exciting and tangible evidence not only of the might but of the good will of the United States."

England and France had elected the American navy and country to their club. French Admiral Gervaise hailed the cruise as "the greatest feat of naval maneuvering ever undertaken in time of peace." With sophisticated criticism, both countries had seen many things wrong with Sperry's ships, but they had been subsequently impressed with new vessels being commissioned or on the way—the 20,000-ton *Delaware,* for example, "the world's most powerful battleship", and the *North Dakota,* both with ten 12-inch cannon, and submerged torpedo tubes. Almost equal in power were the 16,000-ton *South Carolina* and *Michigan,* both qualifying to be classed as dreadnoughts. Though its position was still disputed (in England by Lord Brassey's highly regarded *Naval Annual,* among others), the United States Navy almost certainly ranked second in the world, grimly adequate to its unforeseen but critical role in the Great War that was rolling towards it like a tidal wave.

One consequence of the cruise was inescapable. It had not started, but it had greatly stimulated a naval armaments race throughout the world. Well in the lead, Great Britain that summer paraded the greatest number of warships (149) ever assembled, up the Thames to London in a saber-rattling display. Robert A. Hart notes that Britain and Germany "each had nine dreadnoughts building by the end of the year . . . Russia appropriated money for five battleships and Spain for three. Italy began four, Sweden three, and Argentina, Chile, and Portugal ordered two a-piece." Roosevelt, quoted *Current Literature* for March 1909, had "rendered the battleship the symbol of modern civilization," and "naval power is now the true test of greatness in a land."

In Asia the American show of force had stimulated the militarists and big-navy advocates, as opposed to the pro-American forces in Japan, and fostered rather than restrained that country's rise to its formidable position in World War II. At the same time, Japan had, during the American cruise, negotiated a secret treaty with Russia that would give both nations a free hand in their respective "spheres of influence," strengthening Japan's position in the Far East, and Russia's position on the mainland.

Roosevelt was undoubtedly sincere when he said, "The most important service that I rendered to peace was the voyage of the battle fleet around the world." It is one of the ironies of history that subsequent events, some fortified by the White Fleet's cruise, led to ever bigger navies that must inevitably clash. The immediate effects of the cruise were generally favorable to America; the ultimate effects had overtones of tragedy, perhaps already unavoidable.

But when all is said and done, the cruise accomplished something that Americans could by and large be grateful for. It had roused the navy from its post-Civil War torpor to a position second only to that of Great Britain. It had roused the country from a narrow interest in its own concerns to a broader interest in the world's affairs. Almost overnight, we had become a major, influential power. It was not a height from which we could look complacently upon the world, but one which challenged our handling of the future.

Today, in the light of world conditions, the voyage of the Great White Fleet and the thinking behind it may seem as obsolete as yesterday's battleships. Saber-rattling and armament displays, though still unhappily existent, are a generally discredited form of diplomacy. A nation is no longer truly measured by its military might. Discredited, too, among most major powers is the belief that force is a means of preserving peace. Rather, we hope for reasonable arbitration—preferably not beneath the threat of naval guns or intercontinental missiles.

But the individual components that went into the achievement of the Great White Fleet are still pertinent. The organization, the discipline, the navigational expertise, of the epochal cruise help even today to convince us that nothing is impossible to a united people dedicated to a common cause. A modern Apollo moon shot, for example, commands the same high regard for responsible organization and scientific efficiency, plus the same cooperation among personnel.

Only the goal is different. We think, or hopefully we begin to think, more of space exploration, more of social justice, more of ecology than we do of threatened conflict with our neighbors. We believe that almost anything *can* be done. Perhaps, in that spirit, the voyage of the Great White Fleet continues to remind us that it couldn't be done but they did it.

Bibliography

Except for Robert Hart's excellent volume, noted below, and the two accounts by Franklin Matthews and Roman Miller, there are few or no books devoted exclusively to the Great White Fleet's cruise. Hence the list which follows consists of supplementary reading, which may often mention the fleet's voyage, its purpose and consequences, but in general gives background material against which to see the cruise in full perspective. Needless to say, the books on Theodore Roosevelt himself are numerous, but neither his letters nor autobiography offer a great deal on the cruise.

BEALE, H. K. *Theodore Roosevelt and the Rise of America to World Power*. Baltimore: John Hopkins, 1956. (Also published by Collier in paperback).

COONTZ, R. E. *From the Mississippi to the Sea*. Philadelphia: Dorrance, 1930. This autobiography of the executive officer of the *Nebraska* gives his personal reminiscences of the cruise.

EVANS, R. D. *An Admiral's Log*. New York: Appleton, 1910. In the four concluding chapters Evans gives his account of the voyage to the Pacific, after which he withdrew from the cruise.

GLEAVES, ALBERT. *Life of an American Sailor: Admiral W. H. Emory*. New York: Doran, 1923. Two good chapters on the cruise, especially from an officer's standpoint, based largely on Emory's letters.

HARBAUGH, WILLIAM H. *Power and Responsibility*. New York: Farrar, Straus & Cudahy, 1961. (Also published in paperback under the title, *The Life and Times of Theodore Roosevelt*).

HART, ROBERT A. *The Great White Fleet.* Boston: Little, Brown, 1965. An objective and thorough account of the fleet's cruise.

KING, E. J. *Fleet Admiral King.* New York: Norton, 1952. King was still at the Naval Academy at the time of the cruise, but his autobiography gives a good naval history of the period.

LORD, WALTER. *The Good Years.* New York: Harper, 1960. Fascinating human interest account of the Roosevelt era, with one chapter devoted wholly to the White Fleet's cruise.

MATTHEWS, FRANKLIN. *With the Battle Fleet.* New York: Huebsch, 1909.

———. *Back to Hampton Roads.* New York: Huebsch, 1909. Both books are based on Matthews' dispatches to the New York *Sun,* and while they give a first-hand account of the cruise they are highly colored for propaganda purposes.

McCALEB, W. F. *Theodore Roosevelt.* New York: Boni, 1931. A good biography of the man and his times, but touches only briefly on the cruise.

MILLER, ROMAN J. *Around the World with the Battleships.* Chicago: McClurg, 1909. Another first-hand account of the cruise as seen through rose-colored glasses.

POTTER, ELMER B. *The United States and World Sea Power, 1908.* Englewood Cliffs: Prentice-Hall, 1955. A thorough analysis, by several authorities, on the position of the United States Navy at the time of the world cruise.

ROOSEVELT, THEODORE. *An Autobiography.* New York: Scribner's, 1929. Roosevelt devotes one chapter to his feelings about the cruise and its purpose.

TUCHMAN, BARBARA W. *The Proud Tower.* New York: Macmillan, 1966. Little about the cruise itself, but an excellent picture of world conditions before, during, and after the voyage.

Index.